Handguide to the Future

A Guidebook for Interpreting the Signposts on the Road to New Jerusalem

Terry Lyttle

Copyright © 1996 by Terry Lyttle

All rights reserved
Printed in the United States of America
International Standard Book Number: 1-883928-17-6
Library of Congress Catalog Card Number: 95-082161

This book or parts thereof may not be reproduced in any form without permission of the author.

Unless otherwise noted, all Scripture quotations are from the King James Version of the Bible. Personal emphasis, noted by italics, has also been added in various verses.

Scripture quotations marked (NIV) are taken from the *Holy Bible, New International Version* ®. NIV ®. Copyright © 1973, 1978, 1984 by International Bible Society. Used by permission of Zondervan Publishing House. All rights reserved.

Scripture quotations marked (NAS) are from the NEW AMERICAN STANDARD BIBLE Copyright, The Lockman Foundation 1960, 1962, 1963, 1968, 1971, 1972, 1973, 1975, 1977 Used by permission.

Published by:
Longwood Communications
397 Kingslake Drive
DeBary, FL 32713
904-774-1991

To contact author:
Terry Lyttle
5114 PT. Fosdick Dr. N.W.
E-128
Gig Harbor, WA 98335
FAX: (206)857-7146

Dedication

This book is dedicated to my wife and best friend, J'Anna; to my father, whose faith and enthusiasm in the project was a constant encouragement; and to Pop and Honey, whom God has blessed in so many ways.

Acknowledgements

I want to give special thanks to Murray Fisher—Dick Sleeper—Dana Shafer—Kurt Kessel—and Mary Ellen Petrilla. These people are real professionals whose God-given talents I appreciate and admire so much. Thank you all!

Table of Contents

Introduction..9

1. The Rapture...11
   The Blessed Hope
   The Doubters
   But the Word *Rapture* Isn't in the Bible
   Rapture Positions
   Setting the Date of Christ's Return
   How Long Is "This Generation?"
   How Close Are We?

2. Signs of the Second Coming 26
   Curiosity
   End-Time Questions of Speculation
   Posttribulation Rapture Signs
   Pretribulation Rapture Signs
   The Revealing of the Antichrist
   How Will We Identify the Antichrist?

3. Revealing of the Antichrist in Daniel's
   Seventieth Week....................................55
   Israel Refused to Listen
   The Babylonian Captivity
   The Fall of Babylon
   Daniel's Seventy Weeks
   Seventy *Shebuahs*
   Sixty-Nine Weeks
   The Seventieth Week

4. Resurrection, Outtranslation, and Glorification 73
   His Precious Promises
   From Hades to Heaven
   Souls and Spirits in Heaven
   Resurrection
   Outtranslation
   Glorification
   A Glimpse at Christ's Glorified Body
   Our Heavenly Bodies

5. The Closing of This Age 98
   The Three Millennial Views
   Is the World Getting Better?
   Who is Really Winning?
   Two White Horses Traveling in Opposite Directions
   Humanity Must Choose
   A Call to Armageddon
   The End of This Age

6. Millennial Transition 114
   No White Throne Judgment for These Two!
   Satan Bound for a Thousand Years
   A Great Reduction in The World's Population
   Wilt Thou Restore the Kingdom to Israel?
   Thy Kingdom Come, Thy Will Be Done

7. The Millennium......126
   A Millennium of Ease?
   Who Will Be King of Israel?
   Millennial Government
   Restoration of the Davidic Kingdom

Does God Love the Jew More Than the Gentile?
The Twenty-Four Elders
Works with Right Motives
Ruling with a Rod of Iron
Life in the Millennium
The Millennial Temple
The Temple Gates
Feast of Tabernacles

8. Satan Is Loosed "A Little Season" 150
   After the Millennium
   Satan Is Set Free
   The Final War
   Gog and Magog
   Satan Cast into the Lake of Fire
   The Great White Throne Judgment
   Two Resurrections and Two Deaths
   Why the Judgment?
   The Judgment
   Do We Care?

9. New Heaven and Earth 167
   Long Road of Time and Change
   New Heaven and Earth
   Will We Remember Our Previous Lives?
   What An Experience!
   Interjection of Warning
   Back to John's Experience

10. New Jerusalem 180
    New Jerusalem: Heavenly Bride or Eternal City?
    God Shall Live with His People

Angels Will Be There Too!
New Jerusalem
Measuring the City
The Gates of the City
Twelve Foundation Theory
The Foundations of Faith
The Twelve Foundations
God's Glory Fills the City
The River of Life
The Tree of Life
Developing the New Earth
No More Curse
Outside Are Dogs
Behold, I Knock at the Door

11. Pretribulation Rapture 202
Pretribulation Rapture
Escaping God's Wrath
Escaping the Trial of Tribulation Saints
A Two-Stage Second Coming
Revealing of the Antichrist
Noah and Lot
The Twenty-Four Elders
Church Not on Earth during the Great Tribulation

12. Midtribulation Rapture 216
When Does God's Wrath Begin?
Three and One-Half Year Great Tribulation
Opening of the Sixth Seal
Revealing of the Antichrist
A Satan Incarnate Antichrist?

13. Posttribulation Rapture 232
    Seal of Divine Protection
    Church on Earth during the Great Tribulation
    No Distinction between Saints
    Distinction between Believers and Nonbelievers
    A Great Multitude Which No Man Could Number
    The Seventh Trumpet
    In Closing
    Heavenly Mindedness

Notes 251

Introduction

Welcome to *Hand Guide to the Future*. This book has been written to educate, bless, entertain, and give hope to the body of Christ. I also recommend that it be shared with friends and relatives who haven't yet made a decision for Christ.

In today's church there is a great excitement and fascination with prophecy, and so there should be. People want to know about the future of mankind, and the answers cannot be found on the psychic hot line or in the mystic's crystal ball. God is the only one who has seen His creation from beginning to end, and within the pages of the Bible, He graciously shares man's destiny — the good, the bad, and the ugly. Of course, the true "hand guide to the future" is God's Holy Word, but the reader can be assured that this book is based solely upon His Word.

Join me in an exploration of prophetic events leading to eternity, then eternity itself. We will begin with the Rapture. What attitude should believers have concerning this event? Is date-setting Christ's Second Coming scriptural? The last three chapters of this book will give a fair critique of the three premillennial rapture positions: pretribulation, midtribulation, and posttribulation.

We will discuss definite, not speculative, biblical signs relating to the Second Advent of Jesus Christ. Many Christians do not understand terms such as *resurrection, outtranslation,* and *glorification.* Neither do they understand how these words relate to their lives. *Hand Guide to the Future* not only defines these terms, but it describes what the believer's eternal body may be like.

The book will take a look at the closing of this age, the dawning of a new age — the thousand-year millennial reign of Jesus Christ. Before moving into eternity, the saddest event in history will be examined: the Great White Throne Judgment. We will talk about how this judgment of damnation should stir our hearts to greater concern for the lost. We will then proceed on to the splendor and glory of eternity: new heaven, new earth, and New Jerusalem.

This book will be different from any prophecy book you have read — and I pray you will have as much enjoyment reading, as I did writing.

Terry Lyttle

Chapter One

THE RAPTURE

The Blessed Hope

Jesus Christ had just fulfilled His earthly ministry: proclaimed to the world who He was; prepared His disciples to take the gospel into all the world; allowed Himself to be sacrificed for the sins of humanity; was resurrected and glorified — now it was time for His departure. The Lord led the apostles and about 120 brethren to the top of Mount Olivet. These faithful believers were given some final instructions—and then:

> And when he had spoken these things, while they beheld, he was taken up; and a cloud received him out

of their sight. And while they looked stedfastly toward heaven as he went up, behold, two men stood by them in white apparel; Which also said, Ye men of Galilee, why stand ye gazing up into heaven? this same Jesus, which is taken up from you into heaven, shall so come in like manner as ye have seen him go into heaven. (Acts 1:9–11)

As these privileged Christians stood atop the Mount of Olives and stared into an empty sky, two angels (who were manifested as men) reaffirmed the promise Christ Himself had made. The promise of a Second Advent, when the Lord would personally return for the church.

In my Father's house are many mansions: if it were not so, I would have told you. I go to prepare a place for you. And if I go and prepare a place for you, I will come again, and receive you unto myself; that where I am, there ye may be also. (John 14:2–3)

Beyond the faithful Christian commitment lies the continuing inspirational promise of Christ's Second Coming. Every Christian generation that has come and gone since this promise was annunciated has believed it would see the return of Jesus Christ. Even first-century Christians were confident they would experience the Rapture. This is made evident by James, the half-brother of Jesus.

You too be patient; strengthen your hearts, for the coming of the Lord is at hand. (James 5:8 NAS)

For almost two thousand years, Christians have believed in the imminency of Christ's return. Peter warned "in the last days" mockers and scoffers would use this unfulfilled promise to ridicule the Christian faith.

The Rapture

> Knowing this first, that there shall come in the last days scoffers, walking after their own lusts, And saying, Where is the promise of his coming? for since the fathers fell asleep, all things continue as they were from the beginning of the creation. (2 Peter 3:3–4)

Mockers and scoffers, who proudly wear their ignorance like royal robes, completely miss the significance of having a perpetual state of expectancy concerning the Second Advent. If Christ had told the apostolic church He would return, but not for two thousand years, many would have lost zealousness and a spirit of lethargy would have permeated the church. How would you feel if your employer said, "Sure I'll pay you. How about Thursday of next year?"

Living without the "blessed hope" alive in one's life, without the belief Christ will soon rapture His church, without the fiery inspiration and faith-building qualities this hope produces would kill the very thing Jesus wanted kept alive in the hearts and minds of His people. A Christian whose eyes are focused on heaven and whose heart's desire is to see the Lord is a faithful servant and a committed believer.

> Looking for that blessed hope, and the glorious appearing of the great God and our Saviour Jesus Christ. (Titus 2:13)

The Doubters

Second Peter 3:3–4 warned that scoffers would arise in the last days and attack the "blessed hope." We would expect this heathenistic attitude from Christ-rejecting atheists, but sadly, it is professing Christians who are the main antagonists of a literal rapture of the church. In spite of more than three hundred New

Testament references directly pertaining to the Second Coming, liberal theologians and some evangelicals either allegorize these verses or deny divine inspiration by saying these are just the hopeful words of mere men. The following Associated Press news article proves quite revealing:

> Scholars say:
> Jesus didn't promise to return.
> According to a recent Associated Press article, a group of biblical scholars has agreed that Jesus Christ never promised to return to earth. About 100 scholars, theologians and historians discussed the teachings of the historical Jesus in a recent three-day seminar and concluded that the gospel writers and later followers of Jesus were the ones who predicted a Second Coming of Christ.
> Robert Funk, a "New Testament expert" and seminar founder, said that most of its members believe that Jesus was just a wandering sage and did not think of himself as divine, "although he felt very close to God."
> The seminar's findings reflect what is being taught in most universities and seminaries today, said the Rev. Edward F. Beutner, a Jesuit and campus minister at Santa Clara University and seminar member. "These are not maverick scholars," Beutner said. "They take a very careful approach to how sayings of Jesus were transmitted and to the evolution of the Bible texts."[1]

Libertine theologians are often presented to public as biblical scholars and as spokesmen for the church. Calling them "Bible scholars" is a gross misnomer, a travesty of enormous proportions. But what is even more heart-wrenching is the fact

The Rapture

that most universities and seminaries are seducing our young men and women away from the inspired, infallible, holy Word of God. Students are being systematically poisoned by heretics who deny the Second Coming, the virgin birth, the deity of Christ, the Trinity, the resurrection, and even the crucifixion itself. Once the authenticity, reliability, and inerrancy of Scripture is questioned or denied, spiritual truth becomes subjective and relative, as opposed to objective and absolute.

The Church cannot afford to sit idly by while the tenets of true Christian faith are postulated as lies, myths, half-truths, and legends. Jesus told Peter the gates of hell shall not prevail against the church; but it's important to understand that when the Lord said this, He wasn't giving a blanket promise covering everything from soup to nuts. The gates of hell will not prevail against God's faithful. But it is naive to think that Satan doesn't make inroads into the lives and spirituality of those "professing Christians" who throw out the welcoming mat of accommodation and compromise—those who choose to travel the road of apostasy.

Today, the word *Christian* has come to mean practically anything. It's getting to the point that when someone asks, "Are you Christian?" the term must be defined. For example, the other day a young man confessed being a Christian. He was part of a group called the "First Church of New Thought," which combined new age philosophy with a convoluted form of Christian theology. In talking with him, it became quite obvious that the "First Church of New Thought" doesn't spend much time thinking!

While the Bible does contain allegories, hyperboles, and metaphors, a literal approach to interpretation should always be taken unless the context demands otherwise. This hermeneutic (i.e., rule of interpretation) protects against *eisegeses*, which means reading into the text preconceived ideas. It safeguards against false doctrine. Freewheeling allegorization reduces meaning to private interpretation, which violates Scripture. The Bible states, "No prophecy of the scripture is of any private interpretation" (2 Peter 1:20).

There is no basis for spiritualizing the verses that speak of the Second Advent. When Jesus Christ said He would return for His church, that's exactly what He meant. We don't need to squint our eyes, go into a trance, or filter His words through a metaphysical haze!

But the Word *Rapture* Isn't in the Bible

Those who deny a literal rapture often use the myopic argument that the word *rapture* does not appear in Scripture. *Rapture, Trinity,* and *Bible* are all words not found in Holy Writ. The fact that certain words are not present in the Bible doesn't automatically disqualify them as biblical terms. It doesn't necessarily invalidate the meaning the words represent.

> Then we which are alive and remain shall be *caught up* together with them in the clouds to meet the Lord in the air: and so shall we ever be with the Lord. (1 Thessalonians 4:17)

The Greek word for "caught" is *harpazo*, which means "to snatch away, catch away, pluck up," or "to take by force." In regards to the outtranslation of the saints of God, *harpazo* and *rapture* are synonyms.

Let's say that you read a book on motor vehicles in which only the word *automobile* was used. A friend happens by and you begin telling him about the book, but instead of referring to motor vehicles as "automobiles," you simply say "cars." Now, it would be ridiculous for your friend to look at the book and comment, "This

The Rapture

book is not about cars because it doesn't contain the word *car*.

A day is coming when Old and New Testament believers will literally leave this earth to meet Jesus Christ in the air. *Rapture of the church* is a beautiful way to express this awesome event.

Brethren, don't allow anyone to rob you from believing in and looking forward to the blessed hope. Don't let the eloquent speech of man's wisdom quench the excitement, the anticipation, of soon seeing Jesus Christ. If someone tells you the Rapture is not to be taken literally, politely point them to Scripture that clearly proves a literal Rapture.

The blessed hope is so essential to our Christian faith. We should truly rejoice in its reality and use it as a witnessing tool. The blessed hope of the Lord's return and our gathering together unto Him both comforts and encourages:

When the battle has made you weary,
and life no longer seems fair.
When friends and relatives have failed you,
and you sit in a pit of despair.

Then turn your eyes toward heaven,
for the blessed hope is there.
Don't be downcast or discouraged,
for God sees, He loves, and He cares.

The days are getting shorter,
and the time is drawing near.
One day we'll look toward heaven,
Praise God! It's Jesus! He's here!

(Poem by author)

HAND GUIDE TO THE FUTURE

Rapture Positions

There are three premillennial rapture positions in regards to the Great Tribulation: pretribulation, midtribulation, and posttribulation. The following is the basic foundation for each of these beliefs. The rapture critique presented in Chapters 11 through 13 will delve more deeply into these different viewpoints.

The Pretribulation Position

The pretribulation position is based on the belief that the rapture will occur *before* the Great Tribulation begins. Since most pretribulationists believe in a seven-year Tribulation, they see themselves being removed from earth at the beginning of "Daniel's seventieth week."

The Midtribulation Position

The midtribulation position is established on the premise that the church will be raptured in the *middle* of Daniel's seventieth week. While most midtribers accept the idea of a seven-year "tribulation period," it's important to note they make a distinction between "tribulation," and "Great Tribulation." They see the wrath of God (Great Tribulation) beginning in the middle of Daniel's seventieth week, and the rapture occurring just before this time begins. Midtribers call this a "pre-wrath rapture." This will be made more clear in Chapter twelve.

The Posttribulation Position

The posttribulation position is founded on the idea that the church will be raptured at the *end* of the Great Tribulation. Some posttribers hold to a seven-year Tribulation; others believe this period is three and one-half years.

The Rapture

Each of these differing views are held by biblically sound scholars. This means worthy arguments can be made for each position. However, having said this, let me add that intolerance toward opposing rapture viewpoints is widespread in the church. Sure, statements like, "I'm so pretrib, I don't eat Post Toasties," are funny and innocent. But many influential Christian evangelists, preachers, and teachers go beyond innocent humor by demonstrating no tolerance for rapture views that differ from their own. After reading their literature or hearing them speak, one is left with the impression that only an idiot would believe in a view that is different from theirs. Dogmatism on nonessentials is a form of unwarranted prejudice. It closes the door to open-minded discussion and demonstrates a lack of respect.

Why do brilliant Christian minds disagree on the outtranslation? Because God did not give us a specific rapture date. He allows us to know certain events leading up to the Second Coming, but not the hour, day, month, or year. Different Scriptures, interpreted differently, produce differing opinions. My particular belief is no better than yours, and let's face it: one of us could be right, or we both could be wrong. God doesn't want His children worrying about *times and dates*. Christians need to live each day in full readiness, as if Jesus were returning the next.

> Now, brothers, about times and dates we do not need to write to you, for you know very well that the day of the Lord will come like a thief in the night. (1 Thessalonians 5:1–2 NIV)

> But of that day and that hour knoweth no man, no, not the angels which are in heaven, neither the Son, but the Father. Take ye heed, watch and pray: for ye know not when the time is. (Mark 13:32–33)

Watch therefore: for ye know not what hour your Lord doth come....Therefore be ye also ready: for in such an hour as ye think not the Son of man cometh. (Matthew 24:42, 44)

Jesus Christ is coming for those who are looking for His coming; those who have clothed themselves in His righteousness, who are walking in true Christian faith—who are occupying the land until He comes. The question isn't When will Jesus return? but Are we ready?

Wise Christians put their rapture positions in subjection to a "pan-rapture" perspective: However it pans out, is OK with them! We should all prepare ourselves to go through the Great Tribulation, but even the diehard posttribulationist will not complain if Jesus raptures His church sooner. Let's plant our lives firmly in faith, commitment, servitude, and in God's Word. If we do this, the glorious "blessed hope" will always be alive within our hearts.

Setting the Date of Christ's Return

Is setting dates for Christ's Second Coming a good practice? Is there anything wrong with literature or teaching that purports to know the time of the Lord's return? Setting dates for Christ's Second Coming is not a good practice. Preaching, teaching, and literature of this nature should be avoided for the following reasons:

- Scripture teaches that God is the only one who knows the date of Christ's return (Mark 13:32).
- No date-setting prophecy has ever proven itself to be true.
- Setting dates can be a divisive element within the church.
- False prophecy (i.e., dates that have failed) portray to the world an untrustworthy Christian image.

The Rapture

- The date-setter whose prophecy fails deserves to receive the unsavory label of "false prophet."

Christian prophecy authors and teachers have used various methods for predicting the date of Christ's return. I will refute one of the more popular methods, one that remains alive and well in the church. I call this the "1948-generation" method.

Let's begin with the year 1948. You see, for this method to work one must come up with an end-time birth date. Why 1948? Because this is the year Israel was officially declared a nation. The "1948-generation" date-setter designates this as the end-time birth date because of a misinterpretation of Christ's fig tree parable. Let me quote the parable, then explain what the date-setter derives from the parable and why this is a misinterpretation.

> Now learn a parable of the fig tree; When his branch is yet tender, and putteth forth leaves, ye know that summer is nigh: So likewise ye, when ye shall see *all these things*, know that it [He] is near, even at the doors. Verily I say unto you, This generation shall not pass, till all these things be fulfilled. (Matthew 24:32–34)

The "1948-generation" date-setter declares that the "fig tree" represents the nation of Israel. Just as a fig tree blossoms, Israel blossoms forth as a nation (in 1948) and this begins the official end-time generation, "This generation shall not pass, till all these things be fulfilled." Whatever the individual prophecy teacher perceives as a "generation" is added to 1948, and *voila!* A speculative rapture date emerges.

In refutation, the analogy Jesus draws from the fig tree is not the reestablishment of the nation of Israel. He wasn't giving a spiritualized mystery identifying the exact time when "this generation" began. The fig tree was simply an illustration referring to the context of the Olivet Discourse, centering on the Second Coming.

In the spring when sap begins to flow in a literal fig tree, when new shoots appear and leaves form, we know that summer is near and the harvest isn't far away. In the fig tree parable summer represents the Second Advent, and the time preceding summer, which, of course, is spring, represents the signs leading to Christ's return. Jesus said, "When ye shall see all these things," know that His return is near. What was Christ alluding to when He said "these things"? Israel becoming a nation? Not at all! He was clearly talking about events delineated in the Olivet Discourse: the abomination of desolation, persecution, wars, diseases, famines, false Christs and false prophets, the Great Tribulation, and the preaching of the gospel to all the world.

The "1948-generation" date-setter attempts to cross-reference the fig tree parable with Ezekiel's prophecy about the reestablishment of the nation of Israel. However, Ezekiel's prophecy and Christ's fig tree parable cannot be accurately cross-referenced. Using the parable to set possible dates for Christ's return is an exercise in futility.

We've talked about the fig tree parable and 1948. Let's now address the "generation" aspect of the "1948-generation" date-setting method. This variety of date-setter attaches what they perceive as a "Bible generation" to 1948 which creates an erroneous date for Christ's return.

How Long Is "This Generation"?

In the synoptic Gospels Jesus spoke of a generation that would not end until all things pertaining to this present age are fulfilled:

> Verily I say unto you, this generation shall not pass, till all these things be fulfilled. (Matthew 24:34)

The Rapture

Verily I say unto you, that this generation shall not pass, till all these things be done. (Mark 13:30)

Verily I say unto you, This generation shall not pass away, till all be fulfilled. (Luke 21:32)

When Jesus said, "This generation shall not pass away, till all be fulfilled," He was speaking of the fulfillment of events depicted in the Olivet Discourse. He was not offering a puzzle to be figured out, nor was He indicating specific beginning and ending dates. In this context, Merrill Unger gives a bit of wisdom with his definition of the word *generation*:

Generation: A period of time. Differing as the intervals do in this respect, *generation* could never be intended to mark a very definite period, and must be understood with considerable latitude.[2]

When Christ spoke of "this generation," it is my firm belief that He was referring to the entire church age. And because His disciples asked the specific question, "Tell us, when shall these things be? And what shall be the sign of thy coming, and of the end of the world?" (Matthew 24:3), Jesus responded by giving His church things to watch for. Some of these events are quite ambiguous as far as a certain time frame is concerned. Every generation since the Lord gave this discourse has experienced wars and rumors of wars, conflicts between nations, famines, pestilences, earthquakes, false Christs, and false prophets.

The escalation of these events in our day gives credence to the idea that Christ's return is near, but as we previously noted, even the first-century church believed the signs were designated for them. They had seen wars, famines, pestilences, earthquakes, and false prophets. Earlier, Jews witnessed the defilement of

Zerubbabel's Temple by the Selucid king, Antiochus Epiphanes, and later the destruction of the Herodian Temple by Titus which were forerunners, or types, of a future greater fulfillment by the Antichrist, namely, "the abomination of desolation" (Matthew 24:15; 2 Thessalonians 2:4; Revelation 11:2).

What can we learn from all this? That the "1948-generation" date-setting method is wrong. That no matter what method is employed, setting a date for Christ's Second Coming always results in a contrived date built upon a faulty premise. We also learn that date-setters have one thing in common: they are all false prophets, "For in such an hour as ye think not, the son of man cometh" (Matthew 24:44).

God has chosen to keep the day and hour of Christ's Second Coming a divine secret. However, the church can be assured that we are living in the "generation" of Christ's return—and that the Lord wants the "blessed hope" of His glorious appearance to be a constant inspiration.

How Close Are We?

Although the practice of setting dates for Christ's return violates Scripture and is a foolish thing to do, I imagine the heart of the date-setter is sincere because he or she has a strong desire to see the Lord soon. Isn't this an emotion we all share? The desire to see the Saviour in person; to behold His majesty and glory face-to-face? An interesting question is: In His prophetic teaching, did Jesus give us any clue that indicates His return will be near the time in which you and I live? I believe He did, and I'm also convinced His Second Advent is quickly approaching.

Although it's difficult relating certain things Christ said in His Olivet Discourse to our present time (e.g., wars, rumors of wars, famines, pestilences, earthquakes, false Christs, and false

The Rapture

prophets), He said something very revealing concerning the end of this present age:

> And this gospel of the kingdom shall be preached in all the world for a witness unto all nations; and then shall the end come. (Matthew 24:14)

Today, the gospel of the kingdom has practically blanketed the world. Missionaries carrying the good news have done marvelous things for the kingdom. Christian crusades have won thousands upon thousands of spiritually hungry souls. Television, radio, satellite, and shortwave broadcasts have also covered many parts of the world. The fall of the Soviet Union has opened the door for God's Word, and much fruit is being manifested. Religions that are opposed to the Christian message have built a spiritual barrier, but it's not as though the gospel isn't available to them.

In today's world, it is the rare individual who has not heard of Jesus Christ and the claims of Christianity. There is still much work to be done, but the preaching of the gospel to *all the world* lets us know that we are in the "spring" of Christ's return. The fig tree is about to bloom, which means the summer harvest is just around the corner.

> And when these things begin to come to pass, then look up, and lift up your heads; for your redemption draweth nigh. (Luke 21:28)

Chapter Two

SIGNS OF THE SECOND COMING

Curiosity

By nature, we humans are curious creatures. Curiosity has been the catalyst for seeking knowledge in all spheres of life. In the time of Solomon, people traveled great distances to hear his God-given wisdom, his insights into the world in which they lived.

When it comes to curiosity about the future of man, the Christian has a distinct advantage over the rest of the world. God is the only one who has seen beginning to end, and He has graciously shared a significant amount of this knowledge in the

Bible. Let us curious ones take a look at signs of Christ's Second Coming. This will be presented from two different rapture perspectives: Bible-based signs of Christ's Second Coming from the posttribulation position; and Bible-based signs of the Second Advent from the pretribulation position.

We will begin by briefly looking at four end-time questions of speculation. These are things you may or may not be familiar with, but they are believed to be true by many prophecy teachers and students.

End-Time Questions of Speculation

God's prophetic Word describes many events to occur in the end times. The difficulty lies in correlating these events to what we see happening in today's world:

1. Will Europe become "the whore of Babylon"—the center of the world's wealth and international trade?

> For all nations have drunk of the wine of the wrath of her fornication, and the kings of the earth have committed fornication with her, and the merchants of the earth are waxed rich through the abundance of her delicacies. (Revelation 18:3)

2. Will the ten kings represent the ten core nations of the European Economic Community?

> And the ten horns which thou sawest are ten kings, which have received no kingdom as yet; but receive power as kings one hour with the beast. These have one mind, and shall give their power and strength unto the beast. (Revelation 17:12–13)

3. Will the Antichrist arise out of a united Europe?

And there was given unto him a mouth speaking great things and blasphemies; and power was given unto him to continue forty and two months. (Revelation 13:5)

4. Will the pope become the False Prophet?

And I saw three unclean spirits like frogs come out of the mouth of the dragon [Satan], and out of the mouth of the beast [the Antichrist], and out of the mouth of the false prophet. (Revelation 16:13)

These are intriguing speculations, but it is important to understand that they are only speculations. While these theories are often presented as though they are fact, we must be cautious and realize no one has conclusively proven them. The author personally believes that these four "questions of speculation" are within the realm of possibility. They are certainly things we need to watch. However, we live in a constantly changing world; what seems to fit today may prove to be wrong tomorrow. Many Christians were absolutely sure Adolf Hitler was the Antichrist, but time proved he wasn't.

As time moves us closer to the fulfillment of all things, definite signs will appear, letting the believer know it's time to pack the bags! If the posttribulation rapture is correct, these signs will be in abundance. If the opposing pretribulation rapture is correct, the signs will be limited.

Posttribulation Rapture Signs

As the wrath of God is poured out through the seals, trumpets, and vials, there will be no doubt the Great Tribulation is in progress and the Second Advent is near.

Earthquakes

During the Great Tribulation, several earthquakes occur. Two of these terrible tremors are clearly recognizable. When the sixth seal is opened, the earth shakes to such an extent that every mountain and island is shifted to a new location (Revelation 6:12–16).

If the sixth seal quake were to be described as "the granddaddy of all earthquakes," then the seventh vial quake would have to be called "the granddaddy's daddy." This earthquake is so fierce that every island is absorbed into the sea, every mountain is leveled, and cities throughout the world are reduced to piles of rubble. The destructive magnitude of the seventh vial earthquake is unparalleled in all of history, "a great earthquake, such as was not since men were upon the earth, so mighty an earthquake, and so great" (Revelation 16:18).

Saltwater Contamination

When the second trumpet is sounded, a third of all aquatic life will perish. The remaining two-thirds will expire when the second vial is poured into the oceans and seas (Revelation 8:8–9; 16:3).

Freshwater Contamination

When the third trumpet sounds, one-third of the fresh water supplies will be poisoned, causing the deaths of untold thousands. The rest of the world's fresh water will become undrinkable when the third vial is poured out (Revelation 8:10–11; 16:4–6).

Demon Locusts

One of the more frightening signs of the Second Coming will be when the earth opens up to release hideous demon spirits. Spirits are invisible to the human eye unless they are physically manifested. As the fifth trumpet is sounded God allows demon spirits to be *physically* manifested so they can *physically* torment humanity. These demons will swarm out of the bottomless pit, the abyss, like a huge army of hungry locusts. If you have ever walked through a town as swarms of locusts came through, you have the picture. It will be terrifying!

These demons will probably be a lot smaller than horses, but each will have a horse's body, with a metal breastplate and a metal blanket covering. The head will have the appearance of a long-haired man, with large, lion-type teeth. Their tool of torment will be a stinger resembling a scorpion's tail, which releases some sort of poisonous substance. These denizens of darkness will administer pain as they fly about, propelled by wings that make a furious racket.

What will make the fifth trumpet judgment even more frightening is the thick smoke that will ascend out of the bottomless pit and encircle the earth, even blocking out the sun. Trying to find their way through this dense, smoky fog, people will hear the clamoring wings of these horrible creatures, and by the time their eyes focus in on the gruesome aggressors, it will be too late. The venom from the stinger cannot cause death, but it will make people so ill they'll literally wish they could die.

> And in those days shall men seek death, and shall not find it; and shall desire to die, and death shall flee from them. (Revelation 9:6)

The greatest toxicologists in the world will fail to produce an antidote. The fifth trumpet judgment will last five months. It will only affect those who have not received the protective seal of God.

Signs of the Second Coming

> And it was commanded them that they should not hurt the grass of the earth, neither any green thing, neither any tree; but only those men which have not the seal of God in their foreheads. (Revelation 9:4)

Two Witnesses

A positive sign (at least for Christians) of Christ's Second Coming, will be the ministry of the two witnesses. These individuals will be uniquely identifiable from all other believers, including the 144,000 Christian Jews mentioned in Revelation 7. They will have the uncanny ability to control weather, poison water, and bring any judgment they choose upon the ungodly. And all hostilities toward them will be met with reflective recompense.

> And if any man will hurt them, fire proceedeth out of their mouth, and devoureth their enemies: and if any man will hurt them, he must in this manner be killed. (Revelation 11:5)

Revelation 11:4 refers to these men as "the two olive trees, and the two candlesticks standing before the God of the earth." This allusion to Zechariah 4:3–14 has produced many interesting theories as to the identity of the two witnesses:
- Enoch and Elijah
- Elijah and Elisha
- Moses and Elijah
- John and Moses
- Joshua and Zerubbabel
- Two contemporary Christian Jews
- Two Gentiles (spiritual Israel)
- The two olive trees represent both natural and spiritual Israel, meaning one would be a Jew, the other a Gentile.

Enoch and Elijah head the list of likely candidates, since neither of these men experienced physical death (Genesis 5:24 and 2 Kings 2:11). In addition, the Old Testament closes with the following promise of Elijah's return:

> Behold, I will send you Elijah the prophet before the coming of the great and dreadful day of the Lord: And he shall turn the heart of the fathers to the children, and the heart of the children to their fathers, lest I come and smite the earth with a curse. (Malachi 4:5–6)

Although John the Baptist, the forerunner who paved the way for the Savior's ministry, denied being Elijah (John 1:19–27), Jesus made it clear that John was indeed the *fulfillment* of Elijah's coming in Matthew 11:7–14, Matthew 17:10–13, and Mark 9:11–13.

> And his disciples asked him, saying, Why then say the scribes that Elias [Elijah] must first come? And Jesus answered and said unto them, Elias truly shall first come, and restore all things. But I say unto you, That Elias is come already, and they knew him not, but have done unto him whatsoever they listed. Likewise shall also the Son of man suffer of them. Then the disciples understood that he spake unto them of John the Baptist. (Matthew 17:10–13)

> And he [John the Baptist] shall go before him in the spirit and power of Elias, to turn the hearts of the fathers to the children, and the disobedient to the wisdom of the just; to make ready a people prepared for the Lord. (Luke 1:17)

It is the author's opinion that John the Baptist fulfilled

Signs of the Second Coming

Malachi's prophecy; that the two witnesses will not descend from heaven (e.g., Enoch and Elijah, John and Moses, or Joshua and Zerubbabel), but will be chosen from among those on earth, be they Christian Jews, Gentiles, or a combination of Jew and Gentile.

No matter whom Christ chooses to be His two witnesses, one thing is certain: They will be men of impeccable character, wisdom, maturity, and insight. God would not intrust this awesome power and anointing to just any Tom, Dick, or Harry. Moses spent forty years on the backside of the desert before God saw in him the maturity needed to deliver more than two million Hebrews from Egypt.

The appearance of the two witnesses will be a sign of the Second Advent. And in spite of their ability to bring painful judgment upon the ungodly, and in spite of the fact the world celebrates their eventual death in the style of Christmas (Revelation 11:9–10), their ministry will be quite positive. These men are witnesses for Christ; and when Christ is witnessed, souls are affected.

Scripture says they "shall prophesy a thousand two hundred and threescore days, clothed in sackcloth" (Revelation 11:3). For 1,260 days (or three and one-half years, which some believe to be the length of the Great Tribulation) the witnesses *shall prophesy*. The word *prophesy* means to "speak beforehand," to "tell about the future."

The appearance of the two witnesses will not only be a sign of Christ's Second Coming, but also a sign of God's tremendous grace, love, and patience: "Not willing that any should perish, but that all should come to repentance" (2 Peter 3:9). Lest anyone forget, the Great Tribulation is a time of wrath and temporal judgment. God graciously extends His mercy and fairness to undeserving people by anointing His two witnesses for a portentous ministry: Warning citizens of impending calamities; explaining the whys and wherefores of their present crisis; and offering the only hope they have—salvation through the shed blood of Jesus Christ.

To demonstrate the seriousness and urgency of their testimony, these men are clothed in sackcloth, which indicates Jewish ancestry. The two witnesses will more than likely be Christian Jews. Sackcloth is an extremely uncomfortable, coarse material made from goat's hair. In times of personal or national distress, grief, repentance, or mourning for the dead, the Jews would wear sackcloth, often rubbing themselves with ashes.

Undoubtedly, Christ's witnesses will identify the two beasts of Revelation 13: first beast, *the Antichrist* (Revelation 13:1–10); second beast, *the False Prophet* (Revelation 13:11–17).

The witnesses will also speak out against the whore of Babylon, "MYSTERY, BABYLON THE GREAT, THE MOTHER OF HARLOTS AND ABOMINATIONS OF THE EARTH" (Revelation 17:5). Babylon is described in Scripture as being comprised of two factions. The first is the economic and political system orchestrated by the Antichrist and his ten kings (Revelation 17:12–13). The second is the harlot church, with the False Prophet as mentor of a universal religious amalgamation. A demonic "spiritual counterfeit," antithetical to and hostile toward fundamental, evangelical Christianity.

The two witnesses will warn the nations of the world to refrain from doing business with the Antichrist's economic power structure and be quite explicit in describing the eternal judgment destined for all who willfully succumb to the satanic initiation rite called *the mark of the beast.*

And the third angel followed them, saying with a loud

voice, If any man worship the beast and his image, and receive his mark in his forehead, or in his hand, The same shall drink of the wine of the wrath of God, which is poured out without mixture into the cup of his indignation; and he shall be tormented with fire and brimstone in the presence of the holy angels, and in the presence of the Lamb: And the smoke of their torment ascendeth up for ever and ever: and they have no rest day nor night, who worship the beast and his image, and whosoever receiveth the mark of his name. (Revelation 14:9–11)

If the church is on the earth during the Great Tribulation, the appearance of the two witnesses will be a wonderful sign of the Lord's Second Coming. During this time of persecution, sadness, and hardship, seeing God's magnificent power working through these two brethren will encourage Christians to stand strong in faith, knowing that any sufferings they may have to endure "are not worthy to be compared with the glory which shall be revealed in us" (Romans 8:18).

Pretribulation Rapture Signs

Within the cavalcade of contemporary books on prophecy lies a tendency to practically canonize theoretic assumptions. Sincere Christians have and will continue to put the cart before the horse. This is done by endeavoring to speed up God's prophetic clock by setting dates for Christ's Second Coming and by presenting particular end-time scenarios as foregone conclusions. There is nothing inherently wrong with speculating about the future of mankind or world events as related to Bible prophecy, but problems develop when one graduates "possibility" to "probability," and "probability" to "fact."

The Bible itself is the "sure word of prophecy" (2 Peter 1:19). Unlike the prognosticators, soothsayers, and predictors whose divinations prove to be 100 percent true a dismal 10 percent of the time, the Bible's track record is most impressive: 100 percent true, 100 percent of the time! It never has failed, and it never will fail. When Scripture says the future will bring forth an Antichrist, a False Prophet, 144,000 Christian Jews, two witnesses, a new world order, the War of Armageddon, the millennial reign of Christ, and the White Throne Judgment, the believer can put complete faith in what God has prophesied.

As would be expected, pretribulation rapture signs established upon "the sure word of prophecy" are not as profuse as posttribulation signs. This does not preclude a pretribulation rapture; it just means there are fewer signs.

The ever-increasing rise of wars, rumors of wars, famines, pestilences, earthquakes, false Christs, and false prophets would seem to indicate that we are on the brink of the Second Advent. However, it is impossible to put these tragedies spoken of by Christ into a calculable Second Coming time frame. Graphs can demonstrate fluctuations and drastic rises in such events, but they cannot pinpoint where we are in regards to the rapture.

In 2 Thessalonians 2, we discover that the church in Thessalonica was in a state of quandary over reports saying that the coming of Jesus Christ, the rapture, and the Day of the Lord, had already occurred. The apostle Paul refutes this erroneous report by writing:

> Let no man deceive you by any means: for that day shall not come, except there come a falling away first, and that man of sin be revealed, the son of perdition. (2 Thessalonians 2:3)

Signs of the Second Coming

Paul clears up the issue by disclosing two events that "must" occur prior to the Second Coming of Jesus Christ: the apostasy, and the revealing of the Antichrist.

The "falling away," which is the Christian apostasy, is already in progress. However, the identity of the son of perdition, the individual whom the Bible also calls "the man of sin," "the beast," "the man of lawlessness," and "the Antichrist" has not been revealed.

The Apostasy

The word *apostasy* describes a defection from true faith. The preaching of the gospel to all the world and the Christian apostasy are obvious signs that the Second Coming is near.

Today we see a mass defection from true faith into a defective faith. Counterfeits have been perpetrated upon the Christian church, and many are being seduced by doctrines of demons (1 Timothy 4:1). Heartbreaking as it is, professing believers are flocking to churches that tell them exactly what they want to hear.

> For the time will come when men will not put up with sound doctrine, Instead, to suit their own desires, they will gather around them a great number of teachers to say what their itching ears want to hear. They will turn their ears away from the truth and turn aside to myths. (2 Timothy 4:3–4 NIV)

Christianized gurus cleverly mix truth with lies in a caldron of self-serving deceit, and people cheer with great enthusiasm as they drink the elixir of prosperity. False-faith teachers are always clothed in sheep's clothing; always speaks with conviction and authority (which is referred to as anointing); and Scripture flows from their mouths like rain from a polluted sky. Itching ears are told in order to "get from God," one must "give to God." Of course, giving to God doesn't mean subsidizing missionaries in foreign fields. It doesn't mean channeling resources to the sick, poor, needy, or homeless. What does it mean? It means giving to support the lavish life-style of the spiritual mentor—his media expansion and building projects.

In the prosperity church Christian giving is reduced to a business transaction, while God is reduced to some mystical computer that can only operate within the parameters of certain laws. The law of reciprocity, "the law of give and get," can only be activated by giving donations (preferably sizable ones) to religious pimps who know every manipulation gimmick in the book: coercion, sympathy, and trickery.

Coercion is used by misrepresenting the teachings of Scripture. Sympathy is used by sending out emotional letters of appeal that are often written by marketing agencies or ghost-writers. Trickery is used to finagle funds by sending people prayer cloths, trinkets, water, and oils—all personally anointed by the laying on of hands of the head guru himself!

Many are duped into believing the modern-day "faith movement" (also referred to as the hyper-faith church, word of faith, or prosperity church) is *spiritually* legitimate because some of its leaders produce *spiritual* signs: healings, slaying people in the Spirit, the casting out of demons, and prophetic utterances. Brethren, spiritual power can come from two sources. Jesus wanted this vital truth understood, so He gave this stern warning:

> Not every one that saith unto me, Lord, Lord, shall enter into the kingdom of heaven; but he that doeth the will of my Father which is in heaven. Many will say to me in that day, Lord, Lord, have we not prophesied in thy name? and in thy name have cast out devils? and in

Signs of the Second Coming

thy name done *many wonderful works?* And then will I profess unto them, I never knew you: depart from me, ye that work iniquity. (Matthew 7:21–23)

Yes, it's really true! Satan, the "god of this world" (2 Corinthians 4:4), has the power to masquerade as an angel of light, giving what appears to be godly anointing to Christian heretics. His demonic objective is to seduce thousands upon thousands of believers away from historic, orthodox Christian faith—away from sound doctrine—and to lead them into a supercharged counterfeit. These signs and wonders which are performed using Christian phraseology, such as "in the name of Jesus" or "by the blood of Jesus," affect people emotionally, which in turn substantiates the teachings mentally.

> For such men are false apostles, deceitful workmen, masquerading as apostles of Christ. And no wonder, for Satan himself masquerades as an angel of light. It is not surprising, then, if his servants masquerade as servants of righteousness. Their end will be what their actions deserve. (2 Corinthians 11:13–15 NIV)

In the prosperity church the name of Jesus is wielded like a magician's wand, and faith becomes the potion for whatever the heart desires—health, wealth, power, or prestige.

When the sovereignty of God is ruled by the faith of mere men, when *my* will supersedes *Thy* will, when material gain becomes a sign of godliness, when health and wealth are accepted as attributes of great faith, when pride replaces humility, when human exaltation (or self-esteem) is deemed superior to godly submission and repentance, when positive confession or visualization takes the place of tear-soaked sacrificial prayer, when man views himself as a god (small *g*), as opposed to a sinner (big *S*), the church is apostate!

HAND GUIDE TO THE FUTURE

The following words of prosperity preacher Casey Treat, pastor of the Christian Faith Center in Seattle, Washington, epitomize apostasy:

> The Father, the Son, and the Holy Ghost had a little conference and they said, "Let us make man an exact duplicate of us." Oh, I don't know about you, but that does turn my crank!
>
> An exact duplicate of God! Say it out loud, "I'm an exact duplicate of God!" [The congregation repeats it a bit tentatively and uncertainly.]
>
> Come on, say it! [He leads them in unison.] "I'm an exact duplicate of God!" Say it again! "I'm an exact duplicate of God!" [The congregation is getting into it, louder and bolder and with more enthusiasm each time they repeat it.]
>
> Say it like you mean it! [He's yelling now.] "I'm an exact duplicate of God!" Yell it out loud! Shout it! [They follow as he leads.] "I'm an exact duplicate of God! I'm an exact duplicate of God!" [Repeatedly]...
>
> When God looks in the mirror, He sees me! When I look in the mirror, I see God! Oh, hallelujah!...
>
> You know, sometimes people say to me, when they're mad and want to put me down..., "You just think you're a little god!" Thank you! Hallelujah! You got that right! "Who d'you think you are, Jesus?" Yep!
>
> Are you listening to me? Are you kids running around here acting like gods? Why not? God told me to!...Since I'm am an exact duplicate of God, I'm going to act like God! [1]

Apostasy through Homosexuality

God created man to be with woman, and woman to be with

man. Homosexuality violates this natural order of creation, and thus it is a most grievous sin.

"'If a man lies with a man as one lies with a woman, both of them have done what is detestable. They must be put to death; their blood will be on their own heads.'" (Leviticus 20:13 NIV)

Because of this, God gave them over to shameful lusts. Even their women exchanged natural relations for unnatural ones. In the same way the men also abandoned natural relations with women and were inflamed with lust for one another. Men committed indecent acts with other men, and received in themselves the due penalty for their perversion. (Romans 1:26–27 NIV)

Do you not know that the wicked will not inherit the kingdom of God? Do not be deceived: Neither the sexually immoral nor idolaters nor adulterers nor male prostitutes nor homosexual offenders nor thieves nor the greedy nor drunkards nor slanderers nor swindlers will inherit the kingdom of God. (1 Corinthians 6:9–10 NIV)

Because America once stood strong on morality, homosexuals hid their perversion from the public eye. But the moral decline of our society has propelled the gay liberation movement into the media spotlight. Ungodly degenerates are now hailed as heroes as they militantly come out of the closet, surround themselves with liberal lawyers, and attempt to change the laws and regulations that block their proliferation.

Homosexuality is a blight on society. It isn't something to

be proud of, yet every year Gay Pride Week is celebrated by both homosexuals and heterosexuals alike. How true are the words of Scripture, "Although they know God's righteous decree that those who do such things deserve death, they not only continue to do these very things but also approve of those who practice them" (Romans 1:32 NIV).

Across America—police, fire departments, and city officials give their support and approval by allowing parades of perversion down the main streets of our cities. For the past several years, in the part of the country where I live, the Seattle Gay Pride Parade has been replete with city officials leading the march, along with fire engines loaded with gays (blatantly flaunting their sin), and we the taxpayers are forced to pay for it! Sodom and Gomorrah is within reach, and woe unto this nation when this perversion is given minority status.

Homosexuality is another sign of Christian apostasy. However, please don't misinterpret what is being said. The church door should always be open to everyone, including homosexuals. But the purpose of the church isn't to save people *in* sin; it is to save them *from* sin or *out of* sin—"He whom Jesus sets free is free indeed!" But when someone is led to believe that their ungodliness is good, accepted, or tolerated, there is no conviction or inducement to change. Today we find that many churches have openly accepted homosexuality as an alternate life-style. Some have "fallen away" to such a degree of decadence that they proudly ordain homosexuals as ministers of the gospel. Talk about antithesis! This is apostasy!

Other Areas of Apostasy

Apostasy is a most serious matter. In his letter to the Galatians, the apostle Paul warned that those who preach or follow a foreign gospel—one that is a warped rendition of the

Signs of the Second Coming

original, "Let him be eternally condemned" (Galatians 1:8 NIV). Eternally condemned? Severe words, but understandable when we consider the fact that false doctrine produces perverted concepts of the nature and will of God.

When God's will, Word, and nature is distorted, it results in the preaching of a different gospel, a different God, and a different Christ. This is why the Saviour spoke such strong words to people who use His name, do many things by His name, claim to be Christian, yet at judgment will "indeed" be eternally condemned, "I never knew you: depart from me, ye that work iniquity" (Matthew 7:23).

In Chapter 1, we talked about how liberal theologians came to the conclusion that Christ never promised to return to earth. We read how they perceive the Lord as being nothing more than a wandering sage—a teacher who never thought of Himself as divine. Libertine theology decimates the personality of Jesus, His eternal oneness with the Father and Holy Spirit, His supremacy over all creation. It is, by definition, a different gospel producing a different Jesus. It is apostate!

Apostasy is a definite, observable sign of Christ's Second Coming. Today a plethora of groups have wandered away from the faith, exchanging the truth for a lie, "Now the Spirit speaketh expressly, that in the latter times some shall depart from the faith, giving heed to seducing spirits, and doctrines of devils" (1 Timothy 4:1). Browsing through a book on Christian cults, I was absolutely amazed at the number of counterfeits available to those who "will not put up with sound doctrine" (2 Timothy 4:3 NIV).

Hinduistic New Age Parallels in Apostasy

It is interesting to note that new age philosophy, which has its roots in Hinduism, runs throughout the apostate church.

Being relativistic and contradictory, Hinduism has the liberal flexibility to absorb most spiritual concepts and most religions. It is my opinion that the essence of Hinduism will be the bedrock of the end-time harlot church. For example, parallels can be drawn between the apostate prosperity church and Hinduism.

Parallel between karma and faith: The spiritual law of *karma* is a Hindu belief predicated upon the ideas of good karma, bad karma, karmic debts, and karmic reincarnations. Hindus with "good karma" are prosperous, healthy, and wealthy. They are said to deserve their good fortune because they have good karma. Those with "bad karma" are the poor, sick, and destitute. They deserve their painful existence because of their bad karma.

The prosperity preacher proclaims Christians with big faith, "good karma," stay healthy and gain wealth, whereas Christians with little faith, "bad karma," get sick and have financial difficulties. Because of their big faith, the healthy and wealthy deserve the very best—God's best! And because of their little faith, the sick and needy receive exactly what they deserve. In the prosperity church, suffering and misfortune are often attributed to a deficiency of faith:

- If Christians lack money, they lack faith!
- If Christians lack health, they lack faith!
- If Christians have emotional problems, they lack faith!

The verse that is mangled out of context to support this teaching is Matthew 9:29, in which Jesus says, "According to your faith be it unto you."

Parallel between mantra yoga and positive confession: Hinduism has many forms of yoga including the popular mantra yoga. Mantra is a vocal yoga in which repetitious chanting (repeating the same word or phrase over and over again) is used to acquire the heart's desire.

Signs of the Second Coming

Many in the faith movement use exactly the same technique. For instance, positive confessionists believe that:
- Words create reality.
- Persistent chanting demonstrates faith.
- Faith puts God under obligation to respond.

Positive confessionists have been taught that repetitious chanting demonstrates to God, that they have "the God kind of faith." It is believed that if they just keep confessing "faith words," such as: I am healed in the name of Jesus—I am healed in the name of Jesus—I am healed in the name of Jesus...God has no choice but to heal them. The key, they are told, is to keep repeating positive "faith words" and stay away from negative "doubt words," such as, "pastor, why isn't it working?"

The Bible warns believers to refrain from repetitious prayer that is practiced by pagans: "But when ye pray, use not vain repetitions, as the heathen do: for they think that they shall be heard for their much speaking" (Matthew 6:7). However, the same occultic vocal conjuring methods employed by Hindu pagans is found in the prosperity church dressed in Christian terminology.

In extolling the virtues of positive confession, of how he applied "real faith," a well-known evangelist gave this testimony. Two hours prior to his stage appearance flu symptoms came upon him, so he spent the next two hours chanting, "I'm not sick; I'm healed in the name of Jesus." This phrase was said to be repeated at least five hundred times, then all of a sudden the power of God hit him and took away the flu. In actuality, this evangelist had applied the ancient art of white occult witchcraft, in the form of Hindu mantra yoga, camouflaged in Christian language.

The idea that we can manipulate God through man-made techniques or through the name of Jesus comes from teaching which Scripture refers to as "doctrines of demons." Simply because the name of Jesus is used, doesn't mean Jesus is behind the words or actions of the individual.

> Many will say to me in that day, Lord, Lord, have we not prophesied in thy name? and in thy name have cast out devils? and in thy name done many wonderful works? And then will I profess unto them, I never knew you: depart from me, ye that work iniquity. (Matthew 7:22–23)

The Bible encourages Christians to petition God for their needs, and there is certainly nothing wrong with making requests every time we pray. But turning a prayer session into repetitive incantations, into a chant feast, is occultic.

Parallel between God-realization and we are gods: A major goal in Hinduism is God-realization—developing that spark of divinity inherent to all human beings to the perfected state of self-realization—which occurs when one fully comprehends his own deity.

Prosperity preacher Casey Treat is not the originator of the statement, "I'm an exact duplicate of God." His words and teachings parrot his elder comrades, the big boys of the "faith movement." The basic premise is that since Christians are made in the image of God, that puts them in God's class—we are gods spelled with a small *g*. This not only parallels Hinduism and new age philosophy, but also the cult of Mormonism. But while Mormonism teaches that man may "become" a god—some prosperity ministers proclaim the Christian "is" a god.

The Revealing of the Antichrist

In 2 Thessalonians 2:3, Paul wrote that two events must

occur before the Second Coming of Christ: The apostasy, and the revealing of the Antichrist.

We are indeed in the midst of great apostasy, which indicates that the appearance of the Antichrist is close at hand. No doubt about it, the revealing of the Antichrist will be a major sign of Christ's Second Coming. Although many interesting books have speculated about who the Antichrist may be and where he may come from, Christians can be assured when "Mr. 666" is revealed, there will not be the sound of just one voice howling in the wilderness; instead, the sound of a unified consensus will warn people throughout the world.

This siren of exposure reverberating down the corridors of nations will bring both adversity and persecution upon the church. Most nations will have been seduced by the charismatic pied piper of unity and prosperity. They will not appreciate the church exposing this man for who he really is: a wolf in sheep's clothing, the one Scripture speaks so strongly against.

> And there was given unto him a mouth speaking great things and blasphemies. (Revelation 13:5a)

The revealing of the Antichrist will be successful because the one responsible for his revealing (the supernatural being we call Satan) has done a deviously masterful job in preparing mankind to welcome both the Antichrist and the False Prophet with open arms. He has accomplished this by turning man away from the eternal perfect wisdom and foreknowledge of the Creator to the flawed temporal philosophies of the creation.

> They exchanged the truth of God for a lie, and worshiped and served created things rather than the Creator—who is forever praised. Amen. (Romans 1:25 NIV)

Satan has successfully exploited the fallen nature of man for thousands of years. He has prepared the world for the day when he gives power, position, and authority to the son of perdition. This will result in the event we are discussing, the revealing of the Antichrist.

> And the dragon [Satan] gave him [the Antichrist] his power, and his seat, and great authority. (Revelation 13:2)

The revealing of the Antichrist will usher in the time of sorrows called the "Great Tribulation." However, it's important to understand that God's wrath and judgment is coming because of the rebellion and disobedience of people, not Satan, demons, the Antichrist or the False Prophet. If one should doubt this, then consider the following three questions and their answers:

1. Why do we have apostasy and apostate prosperity preachers? Because the time has come when men will not put up with sound doctrine. Instead, *to suit their own desires*, they have gathered around themselves a great number of teachers to tell them exactly what they want to hear (2 Timothy 4:3–4).

2. Why does 2 Corinthians 4:4 call Satan "the god of this world"? Because the *free will* of man has elected him to office. In their rejection of God and the glorious gospel of Christ, people have allowed themselves to be blinded by every godless philosophy that has come down the pike: humanism, atheism, agnosticism, existentialism, evolution (with its varied theories), cults, the occult—you name it!

> Beware lest any man spoil you through philosophy and vain deceit, after the tradition of men, after the rudiments of the world, and not after Christ. (Colossians 2:8)

3. Why are Satan's two key end-time players (the Antichrist and the False Prophet) going to rise into prominence? Because *people will choose them* to lead mankind into a new era. Scripture says man perishes because of a lack of knowledge—the saving knowledge that is derived from God's Word. Without this knowledge and without the guidance of the Holy Spirit, the world is devoid of spiritual discernment. People cannot accurately evaluate truth: what is of God and what isn't.

> Beloved, believe not every spirit, but try the spirits whether they are of God: because many false prophets are gone out into the world. (1 John 4:1)

Hebrews 11:6 tells us that without "faith" it is impossible to please God and, because of their faithlessness, people will be hoodwinked by both the Antichrist and the False Prophet.

The Antichrist: "Even him, whose coming is after the working of Satan with all power and signs and lying wonders, And with all deceivableness of unrighteousness in them that perish; because they received not the love of the truth, that they might be saved" (2 Thessalonians 2:9–10).

The False Prophet: "And he doeth great wonders, so that he maketh fire come down from heaven on the earth in the sight of men, And deceiveth them that dwell on the earth by the means of those miracles which he had power to do in the sight of the beast; saying to them that dwell on the earth, that they should make an image to the beast, which had the wound by a sword, and did live" (Revelation 13:13–14).

In the poker game of life, it is humanity that has dealt Satan four aces. Fortunately, Jesus Christ is holding a royal flush, and at the end of the Great Tribulation, the Antichrist and the False Prophet will be "royally flushed" into the lake of fire!

And the beast [the Antichrist] was taken, and with him

the false prophet that wrought miracles before him, with which he deceived them that had received the mark of the beast, and them that worshipped his image. These both were cast alive into a lake of fire burning with brimstone. (Revelation 19:20)

But how will the church accurately identify the Antichrist and the False Prophet? The remaining pages of Chapters 2 and 3 are devoted to this issue.

How Will We Identify the Antichrist?

The son of perdition will take control of an economic and political powerhouse—quite possibly the European Economic Community. He will be potentate over ten kings.

And the ten horns which thou sawest are ten kings, which have received no kingdom as yet; but receive power as kings one hour [hour here means a period of time, and should not be taken literally] with the beast. These have one mind, and shall give power and strength unto the beast. (Revelation 17:12–13)

The ten kings will be leaders over ten nations or regions. They will comprise the socioeconomic base from which the world's allegiance is won. The Bible's depiction of the Antichrist, his ten kings, and their kingdoms is that of a whore. Just as a prostitute dolls herself up to lure men into fornication, the "mother of harlots" will be adorned in wealth. And this wealth will entice the nations of the world into a bed of deception, where they will perform economic intercourse with the harlot, "with whom the kings of the earth have committed fornication, and the inhabitants of the earth have been made drunk with the wine of her fornication" (Revelation 17:2).

Signs of the Second Coming

The Antichrist and the False Prophet will effectively reach the world with the attractive concepts of global unity, interdependence, peace, prosperity, religious harmony—the brotherhood of man. The problem with this pretty package is that it doesn't take into account God's prophetic Word, man's fallen nature, Satan's influence, and his end-time agenda. Man in his own effort can never create utopia, and no form of theocracy will work until Christ establishes His millennial kingdom.

The close relationship between the Antichrist and the False Prophet is another factor that will help in making a positive identification. Revelation 13:11 says that the False Prophet will have two horns "like a lamb" and will speak "as a dragon." Horns denote power, and the word *lamb* represents meekness and gentleness. The False Prophet will be a powerful spiritual leader who comes across as piety incarnate. However, his haloed countenance and his religious demur will be in direct conflict with his message. His words will reflect the will of the dragon (Satan) and the goals of the first beast (the Antichrist). The *words* and the *goals* will be hostile toward fundamental, evangelical Christianity—diametrically opposed to the will of God.

Following the preparation done by John the Baptist, Jesus came on the scene preaching the gospel of the kingdom of God, a new dispensation. He performed signs and wonders in order to substantiate both who He was and the truth He brought. His deity was further validated by His death, burial, resurrection, and ascension. Satan will counterfeit the miracles of Jesus by giving great supernatural power to the False Prophet. The False Prophet will use this power in three distinctive ways:

1. To authenticate the Antichrist's message (Revelation 13:4–5).

2. To glorify the Antichrist (Revelation 13:14).
3. To deceive the whole world (Revelation 13:14, 19:20).

Count the Number of His Name

In Revelation 13:18 we find a rather interesting puzzle specifically given for the purpose of identifying the Antichrist. I believe the interpretation I'm about to present deserves serious consideration—it seems to fit perfectly. But until "Mr. 666" is revealed, it must be understood as a theory.

> Here is wisdom. Let him that hath understanding count the number of the beast: for it is the number of a man; and his number is Six hundred threescore and six. (Revelation 13:18)

Notice that the Scripture says "count" the number of the beast—it is the number of a "man"—and his number is "666." The beast (the Antichrist) is a man. His number is 666, and his name is derived by counting his number.

Unlike the English language, the Hebrew and Greek languages have numbers that correspond to each letter of their alphabet. This means every Greek word has a numerical value. To find the number of a name, the numbers of each letter in that name must be added together. If a name is not Greek, then one must do a transliteration. For example, my name is Terry:

T	Tau	T =	300
E	Epsilon	E =	5
R	Rho	P =	100
R	Rho	P =	100
Y	Upsilon	Y =	400
			905

Signs of the Second Coming

The number of my name is 905, which means if this theory is correct, my wife can stop worrying—I'm not the Antichrist!

This is the best interpretation of Revelation 13:18 that I've seen, but it does raise some questions:

1. Do we add only the first name? Most people in the Bible don't have last names, such as Solomon, David, Abraham, Paul, and John.
2. It is estimated that one out of every ten thousand names would add up to 666. Of course, other identity signs coupled with the number would eliminate this problem.
3. According to some Greek scholars there is not a Greek equivalent to the English letters *h*, *j*, *q*, and *w*, which would pose problems for transliterating some names. If the Antichrist's name does not contain these letters—no problem!

For those interested in doing transliterations on possible Antichrist candidates, I have included an English-to-Greek translation chart with numerical values.

HAND GUIDE TO THE FUTURE

English-to-Greek Translation Chart
With Numerical Values

A	Alpha	A	=	1					
B	Beta	B	=	2					
C̲	Sigma	Σ	=	200	C̄	Kappa	K	=	20
D	Delta	Δ	=	4					
E̲	Epsilon	E	=	5	Ē	Eta	H	=	8
F	Phi	Φ	=	500					
G	Gamma	Γ	=	3					
H	Has No Greek Equivalent and No Numerical Value								
I	Iota	I	=	10					
J	Has No Greek Equivalent and No Numerical Value								
K	Kappa	K	=	20					
L	Lambda	Λ	=	30					
M	Mu	M	=	40					
N	Nu	N	=	50					
O̲	Omicron	O	=	70	Ō	Omega	Ω	=	800
P̲	Pi	Π	=	80	P̄	Phi	Φ	=	500
P̄	Psi	Ψ	=	700 (as In Psychic)					
Q	Has No Greek Equivalent Has No Numerical Value								
R	Rho	P	=	100					
S	Sigma	Σ	=	200					
T	Tau	T	=	300					
U	Upsilon	Y	=	400					
V	Has No Greek Equivalent and No Numerical Value								
W	Has No Greek Equivalent and No Numerical Value								
X	Xi	Ξ	=	60					
Y	Upsilon	Y	=	400					
Z	Zeta	Z	=	7					

Chapter Three

REVEALING OF THE ANTICHRIST IN DANIEL'S SEVENTIETH WEEK

Israel Refused to Listen

For twenty-three years the prophet Jeremiah warned Israel of God's impending judgment. He pleaded with them of the urgent necessity to repent of their sinful, rebellious ways and to turn from idolatry—the worship of false gods and graven images. Israel refused to listen; their eyes and hearts were blinded by a false sense of security—by greed, lust, physical and spiritual wickedness, and abominations of every variety. Jeremiah was looked upon as a "gloom and doomer," a loud, pretentious voice the Jews found quite annoying. Other prophets who boldly sounded God's trumpet of warning were mocked and ridiculed, their portentous message fell on deaf, backslidden ears.

> And the Lord hath sent unto you all his servants the prophets, rising early and sending them; but ye have not hearkened, nor inclined your ear to hear. They said, Turn ye again now every one from his evil way, and from the evil of your doings, and dwell in the land that the Lord hath given unto you and to your fathers for ever and ever: And go not after other gods to serve them, and to worship them, and provoke me not to anger with the works of your hands; and I will do you no hurt. Yet ye have not hearkened unto me, saith the Lord; that ye might provoke me to anger with the works of your hands to your own hurt. (Jeremiah 25:4–7)

To say God is patient is an understatement. He is the author of patience. Instead of repenting, Israel decided to ride the Lord's train of long-suffering to its very end. They departed the train at a terminal called *judgment*. God said (my paraphrase), "If you ungrateful people want to serve demon deities, if you desire wickedness, I'll give you Babylon—the gateway to false gods and goddesses, of pagan philosophies and immoral practices. However, Babylon will not be yours to conquer and rule. It will conquer Israel, and the Jews will become its servants."

> And this whole land shall be a desolation, and an astonishment; and these nations shall serve the king of Babylon seventy years. (Jeremiah 25:11)

The Babylonian Captivity

In 605 B.C. Nebuchadnezzar, king of the Babylonian

Empire, invaded the Holy Land. The Jews put up a struggle, but without God's protection it was like getting into an ax fight without an ax. Some of the Jews were taken back to Babylon, while some remained in Palestine under military rule. The young prophet Daniel was part of the Jewish entourage taken captive and brought to the mighty city of Babylon. Possessing great wisdom, intelligence, character, and prophetic ability, it didn't take Daniel long to obtain a position of influence. He was respected by both the Jews and the Chaldeans (Babylonians).

Babylon had been built by the Sumerians, who were descendants of Cush and followers of Nimrod. The kingdom didn't reach its impressive glory and splendor until the rule of Nebuchadnezzar (605–562 B.C.). Nebuchadnezzar was determined to build a monument the world would never forget, and he succeeded. Although the Babylonian Empire was steeped in occultism and moral decadence, Babylon itself was a magnificent work of art. According to Herodotus (circa 460 B.C.), the city was built on both sides of the Euphrates River in the shape of a square. Each side was approximately thirteen miles, 1,385 yards, which means mighty Babylon was mighty large. Two huge walls encircled Babylon, making it virtually an impregnable fortress.

Laced with beautiful streets and canals, the city's interior was an immaculate marvel. Houses were built three and four stories high, complete with water and sewer systems. The city was speckled with pagan temples built to honor a multitude of gods and goddesses. These included the temples of Bel, Ishtar, Marduk, and the famous ziggurat, the Tower of Babel. If you were to enter the city from the north through the massive Ishtar Gates, you and your chariot would be cruising on Procession Street. The walls on both sides of Procession Street were decorated with enameled brick, which displayed giant mosaic pictures of lions (representing the god Ishtar), dragons (representing the god Marduk), and bulls (representing the god Bel).

Farther on down this main arterial your eyes would behold one of the seven wonders of the world—the breathtaking "Hanging Gardens." These gardens were built upon rising terraces that incorporated a sophisticated watering system.

The two sides of the city were connected by a very high arching bridge that spanned the Euphrates River. This bridge was constructed in such a way that it could easily be destroyed if escape to either side became necessary. Nebuchadnezzar also had a secret tunnel under the Euphrates River in case of an extreme emergency. This tunnel could be caved in by kicking out certain key points.

Babylon, oh mighty Babylon! Only crazy people with a death wish would attempt to seize your glory. Wouldn't you know it, the Persians were just that crazy—crazy in a crafty sort of way!

The Fall of Babylon

On the night of October 13, 539 B.C., Belshazzar, the last ruling monarch of the Babylonian Empire, threw a lavish shindig for his nobles, wives, and concubines. Concubines were the king's extramarital playthings. A Christian friend's children use to say, "Solomon had 700 wives, and 300 porcupines." Anyway, as a blasphemous insult to Jehovah, the God of the Jewish faith, Belshazzar had all of the sacred golden goblets that had been stolen from Solomon's Temple brought to the party. The goblets were filled with wine, and the guests saluted all of the heathen deities of Babylon. As the king sat on his throne, sipping wine from a holy vessel of Israel, gloating over his shameful sacrilege, a hand supernaturally appeared before his eyes. He watched in terror as the hand moved across the room to a wall where it wrote the following inscription: "MENE, MENE, TEKEL, UPHARSIN" (Daniel 5:25).

> The king watched the hand as it wrote. His face turned pale and he was so frightened that his knees knocked together and his legs gave way. (Daniel 5:5–6 NIV)

Belshazzar didn't know what "MENE, MENE, TEKEL, UPHARSIN" meant, but suspected it wasn't "Congratulations." He called in Babylon's finest occultists to see if they could decipher the strange writing. When the sorcerers, astrologers, magicians, and enchanters failed to produce the interpretation, the queen suggested that the king summon the prophet Daniel.

> Now the queen by reason of the words of the king and his lords came into the banquet house: and the queen spake and said, O king, live for ever: let not thy thoughts trouble thee, nor let thy countenance be changed: There is a man in thy kingdom, in whom is the spirit of the holy gods; and in the days of thy father light and understanding and wisdom, like the wisdom of the gods, was found in him; whom the king Nebuchadnezzar thy father, the king, I say, thy father, made master of the magicians, astrologers, Chaldeans, and soothsayers; Forasmuch as an excellent spirit, and knowledge, and understanding, interpreting of dreams, and shewing of hard sentences, and dissolving of doubts, were found in the same Daniel, whom the king named Belteshazzar: now let Daniel be called, and he will shew the interpretation. (Daniel 5:10–12)

Daniel looked at the wall and immediately understood the meaning. He shook his head and said (my paraphrase), "King old boy, have you ever heard the expression 'I've got good news and bad news'? Well, I've got bad news and worse news! The bad news is your kingdom is doomed; the worse news is *you're* doomed!" The message on the wall was written by God Himself, and here is the interpretation:

> *Mene:* God has numbered the days of your reign and brought it to an end. *Tekel:* You have been weighed on the scales and found wanting. *Peres:* Your kingdom is divided and given to the Medes and Persians. (Daniel 5:26–28 NIV)

Meanwhile, a few miles upriver the Persian army under Cyrus, which consisted of both Medes and Persians, was planning an ingenious strategy that would give them Babylon. They had fought the Chaldeans on several occasions and knew they needed to get inside the city to obtain victory. As stated, Babylon was built on both sides of the Euphrates River. The huge iron gates that allowed entrance from the river (used specifically for commerce) were sunk so deep that anyone attempting to swim under would drown.

And so, in one night the Medes and Persians diverted the entire river, lowering the water level below the gates. This enabled the Persian army to enter and capture Babylon. The city thought to be impervious to invasion had fallen, thus Babylon became part of the united Medo-Persian Empire.

> In that night was Belshazzar the king of the Chaldeans slain. And Darius the Median took the kingdom, being about threescore and two years old. (Daniel 5:30–31)

Daniel's Seventy Weeks

Daniel and the Jewish captives had just witnessed a major

Revealing of the Antichrist in Daniel's Seventieth Week

power shift. They were now under Medo-Persian rule. The heart of God's prophet was deeply disturbed. He was in a depressed state of anxiety, disappointment, and fear. What was going to happen to his people? Would his homeland remain desolate? Would Jerusalem and the temple continue to be in shambles? Would God's punishment go beyond the seventy years prophesied by Jeremiah?

> And this whole land shall be a desolation, and an astonishment; and these nations shall serve the king of Babylon seventy years. (Jeremiah 25:11)

Seventy years! Seventy years! The words kept haunting Daniel's mind. It had been almost seventy years, and God had not revealed Israel's destiny. With eyes full of tears and a heart of remorse, Daniel fell to his knees and prayed one of the most repentant prayers in the Bible.

> The Lord did not hesitate to bring the disaster upon us, for the Lord our God is righteous in everything he does; yet we have not obeyed him. Now, O Lord our God, who brought your people out of Egypt with a mighty hand and who made for yourself a name that endures to this day, we have sinned, we have done wrong. O Lord, in keeping with all your righteous acts, turn away your anger and your wrath from Jerusalem, your city, your holy hill. Our sins and the iniquities of our fathers have made Jerusalem and your people an object of scorn to all those around us. Now, our God, hear the prayers and petitions of your servant. For your sake, O Lord, look with favor on your desolate sanctuary. Give ear, O God, and hear; open your eyes and see the desolation of the city that bears your Name. We do not make requests of you because we are righteous, but because of your great mercy. O Lord, listen!

O Lord, forgive! O Lord, hear and act! For your sake, O my God, do not delay, because your city and your people bear your Name. (Daniel 9:14–19 NIV)

The moment Daniel opened his mouth to pray, God dispatched the angel Gabriel, and Gabriel said to the prophet:

And he informed me, and talked with me, and said, O Daniel, I am now come forth to give thee skill and understanding. At the beginning of thy supplications the commandment came forth, and I am come to shew thee; for thou art greatly beloved: therefore understand the matter, and consider the vision. (Daniel 9:22–23)

Gabriel gave Daniel one of the most amazing prophecies found in the Bible, and it has yet to be completely fulfilled. This prophecy has become known as *the seventy weeks of Daniel.*

Seventy weeks are determined upon thy people and upon thy holy city, to finish the transgression, and to make an end of sins, and to make reconciliation for iniquity, and to bring in everlasting righteousness, and to seal up the vision and prophecy, and to anoint the most Holy. (Daniel 9:24)

Daniel 9:24 gives us an overview of things that must take place during the seventy weeks. Failure to comprehend this passage in its relationship to New Testament verses, such as Matthew 24:15–22, has led some to conclude that Daniel's seventieth week has already been fulfilled. Those who hold to a preterit interpretation are missing something quite beautiful. Gabriel's message to Daniel is a powerful Messianic prophecy. The prophet wanted to know the destiny of Israel, and God graciously told him of two significant events that would concern the Jewish people: Christ's First Coming, when He

Revealing of the Antichrist in Daniel's Seventieth Week

would be rejected by the Jews, and Christ's Second Coming, when He would be received as the Jewish Messiah.

The seventy weeks of Daniel is a Jewish prophecy—*thy holy city, thy holy people*—although we Gentiles, spiritual Jews, are benefactors. Gabriel outlined six things that must happen during the seventy weeks:
1. finish the transgression
2. make an end of sins
3. make reconciliation for iniquity
4. bring in everlasting righteousness
5. seal up the vision and prophecy
6. anoint the most Holy

The first three things (finish the transgression, make an end of sins, and make reconciliation for iniquity) were fulfilled by Jesus Christ on Calvary's cross. He was the propitiation for the sins of mankind. He brought about reconciliation between humanity and deity.

The last three things (bring in everlasting righteousness, seal up the vision and prophecy, and anoint the most Holy) pertain to the end of our present age when Jesus Christ returns and takes His position as Lord of lords and King of kings. Jerusalem will once again become a holy city. The Jews will accept their Messiah. Christ will be anointed ruler over His millennial kingdom, and everlasting righteousness will no longer be legal, but experiential for all of God's people (both Jew and Gentile); and Daniel's *seventy weeks*, his vision and prophecy will be fulfilled.

Seventy Shebuahs

To us seventy weeks means 490 days. But to the Hebrews the word for week, *shebuah*, meant seven years. This means seventy weeks to the Hebrews would equal 490 years not days. Although it can be a bit confusing, this is generally referred to as "weeks of years."

We see an example of this concept of "weeks of years" in Genesis 29. Remember the story of Jacob, Rachel, Leah, and Laban? Laban was the father of Rachel and Leah. Now, Jacob had fallen in love with the beautiful Rachel and had asked Laban for her hand in marriage. Laban said if Jacob would work for him seven years, he would give him his lovely daughter.

When the seven years were almost completed, the marriage took place. Howbeit, wily Laban pulled the old switcheroo. The woman standing next to Jacob at the wedding ceremony, whose face was hidden by a veil, was Leah not Rachel. In the morning after the marriage had been consummated, Jacob was horrified to see it was Leah he had given himself to, not Rachel.

> And it came to pass, that in the morning, behold, it was Leah: and he said to Laban, What is this thou hast done unto me? did not I serve with thee for Rachel? wherefore then hast thou beguiled me? And Laban said, It must not be so done in our country, to give the younger before the firstborn. Fulfil her week, and we will give thee this also for the service which thou shalt serve with me yet seven other years. And Jacob did so, and fulfilled her week: and he gave him Rachel his daughter to wife also. And Laban gave to Rachel his daughter Bilhah his handmaid to be her maid. And he went in also unto Rachel, and he loved also Rachel more than Leah, and served with him yet seven other years. (Genesis 29:25–30)

From reading these verses, we learn Jacob had to work two weeks which is two *shebuahs*, or fourteen years, to acquire his Rachel. One week—seven years for Leah. One week—seven years for Rachel. Daniel's seventy weeks are seventy *shebuahs* equaling 490 years.

Sixty-Nine Weeks

What makes the seventy weeks of Daniel such a unique prophecy is the accuracy of the first sixty-nine weeks, and the approximate two thousand-year separation between the sixty-ninth and seventieth week. The prophecy is actually speaking of two different time periods: a period of 483 years (which is sixty-nine weeks) and a period of seven years (which is one week). Some believe Daniel's seventieth week represents the Great Tribulation; others see the Great Tribulation beginning in the middle of this week. Gabriel separated the sixty-ninth from the seventieth week by first revealing the sixty-nine weeks.

> Know therefore and understand, that from the going forth of the commandment to restore and to build Jerusalem unto the Messiah the Prince shall be seven weeks, and threescore and two weeks: the street shall be built again, and the wall, even in troublous times. And after threescore and two weeks shall Messiah be cut off, but not for himself: and the people of the prince that shall come shall destroy the city and the sanctuary; and the end thereof shall be with a flood, and unto the end of the war desolations are determined. (Daniel 9:25–26)

From the commandment to restore Jerusalem to the time Jesus Christ entered the holy city as Messiah, is seven weeks, and threescore and two weeks. Let's add up these figures and see how many years are being prophesied. Keep in mind a score is twenty, so when the Scripture said threescore it meant sixty weeks.

HAND GUIDE TO THE FUTURE

Seven weeks =	49 years
Threescore =	420 years
Two weeks =	<u>14</u> years
	483 years

According to Daniel's prophecy, 483 years would pass from the commandment to restore Jerusalem to the day Jesus would enter the city as the Messiah. On March 14, 445 B.C., Artaxerxes Longimanus, king of Persia, granted Nehemiah's request to return to his homeland and restore Jerusalem.

> In the month of Nisan in the twentieth year of King Artaxerxes, when wine was brought for him, I took the wine and gave it to the king. I had not been sad in his presence before; so the king asked me, "Why does your face look so sad when you are not ill? This can be nothing but sadness of heart." I was very much afraid, but I said to the king, "May the king live forever! Why should my face not look sad when the city where my fathers are buried lies in ruins, and its gates have been destroyed by fire?" The king said to me, "What is it you want?" Then I prayed to the God of heaven, and I answered the king, "If it pleases the king and if your servant has found favor in his sight, let him send me to the city in Judah where my fathers are buried so that I can rebuild it." Then the king, with the queen sitting beside him, asked me, "How long will your journey take, and when will you get back?" It pleased the king to send me; so I set a time. (Nehemiah 2:1–6 NIV)

On Palm Sunday, April 6, A.D. 32, Jesus rode into Jerusalem, where He was recognized as Messiah by the disciples and those who believed.

And the disciples went, and did as Jesus commanded

Revealing of the Antichrist in Daniel's Seventieth Week

them, And brought the ass, and the colt, and put on them their clothes, and they set him thereon. And a very great multitude spread their garments in the way; others cut down branches from the trees, and strawed them in the way. And the multitudes that went before, and that followed, cried, saying, Hosanna to the son of David: Blessed is he that cometh in the name of the Lord; Hosanna in the highest. And when he was come into Jerusalem, all the city was moved, saying, Who is this? And the multitude said, This is Jesus the prophet of Nazareth of Galilee. (Matthew 21:6–11)

Daniel's incredible messianic prophecy was given some six hundred years prior to Christ's sacrifice, yet it was fulfilled not only to the year, but to the exact day. At first I had some difficulty calculating this 483-year prophecy. From 445 B.C. to A.D. 32 is 477 years, and subtracting one year for the transition from B.C. to A.D. (because there isn't a "0 B.C." or a " A.D. 0") left 476 years.

Four hundred and seventy-six years is certainly not 483 years—which was baffling to say the least. Then I discovered Grant Jeffrey's book, *Armageddon, Appointment with Destiny*, which was helpful in demonstrating how this amazing prophecy works out to the exact day. [1]

In my calculations above, I had based the number of years from 445 B.C. to A.D. 32 on our solar/lunar year of 365 days. However, a Bible year equals 360 days (twelve thirty-day months). We must first multiply Daniel's sixty-nine weeks (483 years) by 360 days:

360 x 483 = 173,880 days

In order to fulfill this prophecy to the exact day, there must be 173,880 days between March 14, 445 B.C., and April 6, A.D. 32 Now let's calculate this same time period using a 365-day year.

1. From 445 B.C. to A.D. 32 is 477 years.

2. Subtracting one year from 477 (for the transition from B.C. to A.D.) brings us to 476 years.
3. Multiplying 365 days by 476 years brings us to 173,740 days.
4. Add 116 leap-year days to 173,740, and you have 173,856 days.
5. Now add 24 days for the period of time between March 14 and April 6, and the total number of days is 173,880.

The sixty-nine-week (483-year) prophecy was fulfilled to the exact day!

Jesus Christ was overwhelmingly rejected at His First Coming, "He came unto his own, and his own received him not" (John 1:11). And five days following His entrance into Jerusalem, He was crucified. "After threescore and two weeks shall Messiah be cut off, but not for himself" (Daniel 9:26). Our Savior was cut off, but not for Himself. He didn't have to come out of eternity and fully experience humanity, but He did! He didn't have to subject Himself to so much jealousy, hatred, ignorance, and pain, but He did! He didn't have to tell people the truth about life and eternity, but He did! And He didn't have to pay our penalty by dying a horrible death so you and I could receive a beautiful life, everlasting life—but thank God, He did!

We have completed the sixty-nine week portion of Daniel's seventy week prophecy. The reason there is an approximate two thousand-year separation between the sixty–ninth and seventieth week is because we are dealing with a twofold messianic prophecy: Christ's First and Second Coming.

Here is an interesting fact to help put this in proper perspective. The last week of Daniel, his seventieth week, is the last seven years of our present age. It begins with the revealing of the Antichrist, and ends with the physical return of Jesus Christ.

Revealing of the Antichrist in Daniel's Seventieth Week

Let's now take a look at the "revealing of the Antichrist in Daniel's seventieth week."

The Seventieth Week

As was stated in the previous chapter, the apostasy and the revealing of the Antichrist are two events that must occur before the Second Coming. We also looked at some characteristics of both the Antichrist and the False Prophet that will help believers identify these two when they appear on the scene. Daniel's seventieth week will begin with a seven-year covenant between the Antichrist and the nation of Israel. This will remove all doubt as to his identity.

> He will confirm a covenant with many for one "seven." In the middle of the "seven" he will put an end to sacrifice and offering. And on a wing of the temple he will set up an abomination that causes desolation, until the end that is decreed is poured out on him. (Daniel 9:27 NIV)

Because modern-day Israel is in a backslidden state, they will blindly enter into a seven-year treaty with the Antichrist. This treaty could be with the *mother of harlots*, which will be the Antichrist's political and economic system; or it could be a treaty with the Antichrist through his position as head of a United Nations group.

The details of this treaty are not presently known, but one thing is certain: Israel will learn the hard way that when you shake hands with the Antichrist, you had better count your fingers! This seven-year covenant will be broken after three and one-half years, when Israel is invaded by Gentiles who are under the Antichrist's command.

But exclude the outer court; do not measure it, because it has been given to the Gentiles. They will trample on the holy city for 42 months. (Revelation 11:2 NIV)

Daniel 9:27 states that the Antichrist will put an end to sacrifice and offering and place abominations on a wing of the temple. He will do this until the end that is decreed is poured out on him.

As Israel is being trampled on by the Antichrist-led Gentiles (during the final three and one-half years of this present age), the temple in Jerusalem will be defiled. This event is known as the *abomination of desolation.*

He will oppose and will exalt himself over everything that is called God or is worshiped, so that he sets himself up in God's temple, proclaiming himself to be God. (2 Thessalonians 2:4 NIV)

Currently, plans are being made to rebuild the holy temple in Jerusalem. When this occurs, levitical priests will reinstate the Old Testament practices of animal sacrifices and offerings. "Mr. 666" will run the Jews out of this temple, making it desolate of Jewish worship. He will also place abomination on a wing of the temple. An abomination in a Jewish temple is an icon representing a false god. We have seen that the Antichrist will proclaim himself to be God, so it is likely that the abomination placed in the temple will be his image— *the image of the beast.* Those who refuse to worship this image will be killed (Revelation 13:14–15).

In Matthew 24 (the Olivet Discourse), Jesus warns the Jews in Jerusalem to flee out of Israel when they see the abomination of desolation standing in the temple.

When ye therefore shall see the abomination of desolation, spoken of by Daniel the prophet, stand in

Revealing of the Antichrist in Daniel's Seventieth Week

> the holy place, (whoso readeth, let him understand:) Then let them which be in Judaea flee into the mountains. (Matthew 24:15-16)

Those who believe that the abomination of desolation has already occurred and that the book of Daniel has no relevancy to future prophetic events need to read Matthew 24:15-22. Jesus told the Jews to flee out of Israel when they see the abomination of desolation spoken of by the prophet Daniel. The following verses prove that the defilement of the temple and the fleeing of the Jews will introduce the Great Tribulation period.

> But pray ye that your flight be not in the winter, neither on the sabbath day: For then shall be great tribulation, such as was not since the beginning of the world to this time, no, *nor ever shall be.* And except those days should be shortened, there should no flesh be saved: but for the elect's sake those days shall be shortened. (Matthew 24:20-22)

(Matthew 24:15-22 can be cross-referenced with Revelation 12:14-17.)

The Antichrist will remain in Israel until God's judgment is poured out on him. An account of this is given in Revelation 19:19-20. The first thing Christ will do when He returns to earth is to cast both the Antichrist and the False Prophet into eternal hell.

When Jesus returns to establish His millennial kingdom, Daniel's seventy weeks will be completely fulfilled. Christ will be recognized as the Jewish Messiah and will be anointed ruler over every tongue and nation. He will bring righteousness to a world that has refused to live right and give everlasting righteousness to those who receive Him as Lord and Savior.

The temple in Jerusalem will again be a holy place that stands upon holy ground. It is from here that Christ will reign, and those who have been resurrected, raptured, and glorified will rule and reign with Him.

> Blessed and holy is he that hath part in the first resurrection: on such the second death hath no power, but they shall be priests of God and of Christ, and shall reign with him a thousand years. (Revelation 20:6)

Chapter Four

Resurrection, Outtranslation, and Glorification

Let's now shift gears and talk about some future blessings God has promised each of His children. Resurrection, outtranslation, and glorification are prophetic bridges spanning the *twinkling of an eye* distance between the temporal and the eternal.

Humans were created with natural bodies suited for a natural world. A world subject to physical laws that demand decay and death. But there is coming a glorious day when the believer's natural body will be transformed into a spiritual body designed to transcend all the laws and restrictions it now must obey. A new eternal body, destined for a new eternal earth.

His Precious Promises

Can you imagine how discouraging the Christian life would be if Scripture didn't promise a resurrection, rapture, glorification, heaven, and eternity? If Christ's tenure on earth was simply to teach a temporal message, to die, be resurrected, then depart with the sentiment, "Hey church, it's been fun! We'll have to do it again sometime. I'm now leaving to be with My Father; you folks just do the best you can with what you have," there would have been no hope.

As it is, the subject or discussion of death is practically taboo in our culture. But if the hope, faith, and peace that radiates from God's eternal promises were absent from Holy Writ, then death would indeed be a most mysterious and terrifying event. The good news is: the central theme of New Testament theology is the Second Coming of Jesus Christ, and the promise of eternal life for every child of God.

> For God so loved the world, that he gave his only begotten Son, that whosoever believeth in him should not perish, but have everlasting life. (John 3:16)

> And this is the will of him that sent me, that every one which seeth the Son, and believeth on him, may have everlasting life: and I will raise him up at the last day. (John 6:40)

> In my Father's house are many mansions: if it were not so, I would have told you. I go to prepare a place for you. And if I go and prepare a place for you, I will come again, and receive you unto myself; that where I am, there ye may be also. (John 14:2–3)

Resurrection, Outtranslation, and Glorification

The more we understand our Christian heritage in the precious promises of God, the easier it is to accept death, whether it's our own death or the passing of a fellow believer. A heavenly minded Christian who has a firm grasp of eternity views death as simply a state of transition—a doorway into a fabulous future with Jesus Christ—the beginning, not the end.

From Hades to Heaven

The human being is either trichotomous or dualistic in nature; meaning we are composed of three parts—body, soul, and spirit (trichotomy), or two parts—body and soul (dichotomy), with the words *spirit* and *soul* being interchangeable. I happen to subscribe to the trichotomous interpretation but consider the issue of little importance. This is being stated for the benefit of those who believe that soul and spirit are "always" interchangeable terms. As you read this chapter and see the words *soul* and *spirit* used together, it's perfectly acceptable to take it from a dichotomist perspective.

> And the very God of peace sanctify you wholly; and I pray God your whole spirit and soul and body be preserved blameless unto the coming of our Lord Jesus Christ. (1 Thessalonians 5:23)

In Old Testament times, the Hebrews lived under the law—an unfulfilled law. They were required to perform sacrifices and offerings as a means of demonstrating faith, obedience, and repentance. However, animal sacrifices were merely a shadow, a *type*, an outward act that pointed toward the cross, but in no way could they replace the supreme sacrifice of Christ.

The law is only a shadow of the good things that are

coming—not the realities themselves. For this reason it can never, by the same sacrifices repeated endlessly year after year, make perfect those who draw near to worship. If it could, would they not have stopped being offered? For the worshipers would have been cleansed once for all, and would no longer have felt guilty for their sins. But those sacrifices are an annual reminder of sins, because it is impossible for the blood of bulls and goats to take away sins....Day after day every priest stands and performs his religious duties; again and again he offers the same sacrifices, which can never take away sins. But when this priest [Jesus Christ] had offered for all time one sacrifice for sins, he sat down at the right hand of God. (Hebrews 10:1–4, 11–12 NIV)

Since Old Testament saints needed Christ's sacrifice for the propitiation of sin, at death their souls and spirits did not ascend into heaven to be with the Father. Instead, they descended into a region of Hades to wait for the atonement. This temporary abode ("holding tank," if you will) is often referred to as "paradise." However, that may be a misnomer. The word *paradise* is used only three times in Scripture and pertains to heaven itself—the paradise of God (Luke 23:43, 2 Corinthians 12:4, and Revelation 2:7).

During the dispensation of law, the Old Testament period, Hades was divided into two "compartments." One part was for those who (because of their faith and belief in God) would be saved by Christ's sacrifice. The other was for those who (because of their ungodly rebellion and unbelief) would be judged at the judgment of damnation, God's Great White Throne Judgment (Revelation 20:11–15). These two compartments were separated by a great gulf—a no-man's-land that could not be crossed. In Luke 16, we see Abraham in the

Resurrection, Outtranslation, and Glorification

"saved" section of Hades, speaking across this great chasm to a rich man sitting in the "unsaved" section.

> But Abraham said, Son, remember that thou in thy lifetime receivedst thy good things, and likewise Lazarus evil things: but now he is comforted, and thou art tormented. And beside all this, between us and you there is a great gulf fixed: so that they which would pass from hence to you cannot; neither can they pass to us, that would come from thence. (Luke 16:25–26)

In the book of Revelation when the apostle John saw our glorified High Priest, his eyes couldn't take it. He fell at the Savior's feet in complete humility. Jesus comforted John with the following words:

> And when I saw him, I fell at his feet as dead. And he laid his right hand upon me, saying unto me, Fear not; I am the first and the last: I am he that liveth, and was dead; and, behold, I am alive for evermore, Amen; and have the keys of hell and of death. (Revelation 1:17–18)

Christ's crucifixion—His atonement—gave Him the "keys of hell and of death." Subsequent to His death on Calvary's cross and prior to His resurrection, our Lord's soul and spirit descended into Hades. He entered the "unsaved" portion of this holding place and preached a sermon to those who had drowned when God flooded the world. (In heaven we will be able to find out exactly what Jesus said to these people!)

> For Christ also hath once suffered for sins, the just for the unjust, that he might bring us to God, being put to

death in the flesh, but quickened by the Spirit: By which also he went and preached unto the spirits in prison; Which sometime were disobedient, when once the longsuffering of God waited in the days of Noah, while the ark was a preparing, wherein few, that is, eight souls were saved by water. (1 Peter 3:18–20)

Jesus then crossed that "great gulf" separating the two sides of Hades, pulled out those keys of hell and death, and set the captives free! He led a jubilant group of Old Testament saints all the way from "Hades to heaven."

Wherefore he saith, When he ascended up on high, he led captivity captive, and gave gifts unto men. (Now that he ascended, what is it but that he also descended first into the lower parts of the earth? He that descended is the same also that ascended up far above all heavens, that he might fill all things.) (Ephesians 4:8–10)

Souls and Spirits in Heaven

Jesus told the thief on the cross, "Today you shall be with Me in Paradise" (Luke 23:43 NAS). And the apostle Paul, speaking of physical death, equated being "absent from the body" to being "at home with the Lord" (2 Corinthians 5:8 NAS). When Christians die, their souls and spirits go into the presence of Jesus Christ. There is absolutely no doubt about that. They will be in heaven (paradise) with both Old and New Testament saints, including Moses, Abraham, Paul, and John. They will also be joyfully reunited with friends and relatives who were believers before they died.

Resurrection, Outtranslation, and Glorification

But here is a truth few Christians know. Just as Old Testament believers were held in Hades until Christ released them, those in heaven are also in a kind of holding state. You see, they have no bodies; so as disembodied spirits (souls), they are limited in activity. Yes, it is beautiful and comfortable; and yes, they are with Jesus. But the glorification of the saints and the issuance of new bodies will not occur until the resurrection of the righteous dead and the rapture of the church.

Resurrection

Christians publicly identify themselves with Christ's death, burial, and resurrection through an outward act demonstrating inward obedience, namely—water baptism. They rise from the water like Jesus arose from the grave to walk in newness of life. But while water baptism is a beautiful, symbolic gesture pertaining to this life, the resurrection of the dead will be a literal transformation into the next.

> And have hope toward God, which they themselves also allow, that there shall be a resurrection of the dead, both of the just and unjust. (Acts 24:15)

The Bible teaches that there will be two resurrections. The first resurrection will be the resurrection of the righteous dead who will stand before Christ at the Bema Seat Judgment.

> For we must all appear before the judgment seat of Christ; that every one may receive the things done in his body, according to that he hath done, whether it be good or bad. (2 Corinthians 5:10)

The second resurrection will be the resurrection of the unsaved dead who will stand before God at the Great White

Throne Judgment.

> And I saw a great white throne, and him that sat on it, from whose face the earth and the heaven fled away; and there was found no place for them. And I saw the dead, small and great, stand before God; and the books were opened: and another book was opened, which is the book of life: and the dead were judged out of those things which were written in the books, according to their works. And the sea gave up the dead which were in it; and death and hell delivered up the dead which were in them: and they were judged every man according to their works. And death and hell [Hades] were cast into the lake of fire [Gehenna]. This is the second death. (Revelation 20:11–14)

The first resurrection, the resurrection of the righteous dead, will occur near the beginning of Christ's millennial reign. The second resurrection, which is the resurrection of the damned, occurs at the end of the Millennium.

> Blessed and holy is he that hath part in the first resurrection: on such the second death hath no power, but they shall be priests of God and of Christ, and shall reign with him a thousand years. (Revelation 20:6)

Christian films, literature, and sermons on the subject of prophecy often place greater emphasis on the rapture of the living than on the resurrection of the dead. While the thought of millions of people suddenly disappearing from earth is an intriguing prophetic reality, it is clearly the dead in Christ who are more privileged. These heavenly brethren desire an eternal glorified body, but presently are being tremendously blessed, living with Jesus Christ in God's beautiful paradise, having a

Resurrection, Outtranslation, and Glorification

soulish ethereal existence. This is something that those who are living at the time of the rapture will never experience.

Some of the Old Testament patriarchs, such as Abraham, Moses, David, and Daniel, have been with Jesus for two thousand years. They undoubtedly are receiving great preparatory teaching concerning Christ's Second Coming, and the thousand-year millennial period. In addition, the dead in Christ will partake in the first resurrection, "blessed and holy is he that hath part in the first resurrection" (Revelation 20:6). The living will be raptured and glorified, but they will not participate in the resurrection.

In 1 Thessalonians 4, Paul said those living at the Second Advent need not worry about those who have died. In this passage, "fallen asleep" refers to those who have died.

> According to the Lord's own word, we tell you that we who are still alive, who are left till the coming of the Lord, *will certainly not precede those who have fallen asleep.* For the Lord himself will come down from heaven, with a loud command, with the voice of the archangel and with the trumpet call of God, and *the dead in Christ will rise first.* After that, we who are still alive and are left will be caught up together with them in the clouds to meet the Lord in the air. And so we will be with the Lord forever. Therefore encourage each other with these words. (1 Thessalonians 4:15–18 NIV)

Some teach that the dead in Christ rise from the grave in a restored body, then are raptured and glorified with the living. However, regarding the saved dead, the resurrection and glorification are synonymous. The dead exit the grave in a fully glorified, not restored, body. They are buried in a natural body and raised in a spiritual body.

> So also is the resurrection of the dead. It is sown in corruption; it is raised in incorruption: It is sown in dishonour; it is raised in glory: it is sown in weakness; it is raised in power: It is sown a natural body; it is raised a spiritual body. There is a natural body, and there is a spiritual body. (1 Corinthians 15:42–44)

Outtranslation

Outtranslation is an idiomatic word that Christians use to describe the resurrection and rapture of the church. The believer will be taken "out" of this world, and "translated" in terms of substance and location. Scripture is abundantly clear that no one can know the date of the Second Coming. Yet the end-time signs do seem to indicate we are at least in the season of Christ's return, "Looking for that blessed hope, and the glorious appearing of the great God and our Saviour Jesus Christ" (Titus 2:13). The following is a description of how the outtranslation will occur.

When it is time for the resurrection and rapture of the church, Jesus Christ will summon an archangel. As we learned in 1 Thessalonians 4:16, this high-ranking angel will give the Second Coming rallying cry "with a shout, with the voice of the archangel." The Lord will then descend from heaven with all the souls and spirits who have been living in God's paradise. Christ will also have *the trump of God*, which is referred to as "the last trumpet."

> Behold, I shew you a mystery; We shall not all sleep, but we shall all be changed, In a moment, in the twinkling of an eye, at the last trump: for the trumpet shall sound, and the dead shall be raised incorruptible, and we shall be changed. (1 Corinthians 15:51–52)

Resurrection, Outtranslation, and Glorification

Whether Jesus descends from the distant regions of outer space or from another dimension (dimensional theory presented in Chapter 8), when the heavenly host enters earth's atmosphere, the souls and spirits of the dead in Christ will be sent back into their graves. It is difficult for our finite minds to fully comprehend how this supernatural event will occur. But just as the spirit of Christ returned to His tomb prior to His resurrection—the spirits of the "dead in Christ" will return to their burial grounds before they are resurrected.

Once these spirits are in their graves, the last trumpet will be sounded and "the dead in Christ will rise first" (1 Thessalonians 4:16). This is the first resurrection—the resurrection of the righteous dead. The Jews once used trumpets to gather people for meetings, just as Catholics and Protestants have used church bells. The trumpet of God will sound to signify the divine gathering of all His children. The dead in Christ had been buried in a natural body, but are resurrected in a spiritual body.

It is sown a natural body; it is raised a spiritual body.
(1 Corinthians 15:44a)

The first resurrection should not be thought of in terms of an old Gothic horror story. You know, midnight at the old artificially fogged graveyard, where a hand suddenly pops out of the grave, wiggles a bit, then the rest of the body slowly creeps out to the tune of some rather eerie music, dirt dripping from the rising corpse. The glorified body will not be soiled, for the first resurrection will happen "in the twinkling of an eye" —no time for theatrics!

Subsequent to the resurrection, the living in Christ will be raptured. When the last trumpet is sounded, Christians from every walk of life, from every country in the world, will rise to meet Jesus Christ in the air, "we who are still alive and are left will be caught up with them in the clouds to meet the Lord in the air."

Will Christians hear a literal trumpet sound like ancient Roman trumpets introducing gladiators and chariot races? Or will the trumpet blast actually be a sweet voice of assurance heard in the consciences of believers as a preparatory sign? Will God's people hear anything at all? These are intriguing questions, but questions that cannot be answered until the Savior comes for His church.

The resurrection, outtranslation, and glorification will be the most exhilarating events the believer will ever experience. The dead in Christ will rise from the grave in a spiritual body, followed by the rapture of the living. The entire church will float on clouds of glory, beholding the majesty of our Lord and Savior. We will all experience the incredible, euphoric feeling of hovering together high above the earth, cradled in the loving hands of God.

Glorification

There is a well-known evangelist who ends his daily national radio program by saying, "You don't have any trouble; all you need is faith in God." I've heard other evangelists and ministers express the same misleading notion, and I have wondered what kind of fantasy world these guys live in! A trouble-free existence certainly isn't present in their lives, and it will never be present in ours no matter how much faith we think we have. I wish that these neo-high-tech faith, positive confession, self-esteem, possibility-probability preachers would stop giving Christians an illusionary perception of what faith is all about.

Resurrection, Outtranslation, and Glorification

True, God does help His children endure all difficulties. But the fact is suffering, hard times, trials, tribulation, troubles, disappointments, heartaches, obstacles, and persecution are all *by-products* of faith. They simply come with the territory. And the idea that we can somehow pump ourselves up with bigger faith so the negatives of life can be avoided is an unscriptural delusion promulgated by heretics.

> Beloved, think it not strange concerning the fiery trial which is to try you, as though some strange thing happened unto you: But rejoice, inasmuch as ye are partakers of Christ's sufferings; that, when his glory shall be revealed, ye may be glad also with exceeding joy. (1 Peter 4:12–13)

> And when they had preached the gospel to that city, and had taught many, they returned again to Lystra, and to Iconium, and Antioch, Confirming the souls of the disciples, and exhorting them to continue in the faith, and *that we must through much tribulation enter into the kingdom of God.* (Acts 14:21–22)

> And not only so, but we glory in tribulations also: knowing that tribulation worketh patience; And patience, experience; and experience, hope: And hope maketh not ashamed; because the love of God is shed abroad in our hearts by the Holy Ghost which is given unto us. (Romans 5:3–5)

Jesus is the Paradigm of faith—our pattern and example. He suffered in many ways, which means you and I will also suffer. No matter how much faith, power, prestige, or money people have, they don't get a free ride! They don't get through this life unscathed! Many of God's people suffer with congenital problems, degenerative conditions, paralytic difficulties, blindness—acute, chronic, and terminal diseases. Even if one is fortunate enough to escape these debilitating problems, Satan still has a Pandora's box of emotions he joyfully releases: mental and emotional woes, stress, loneliness, anguish, grief, heartache, worry, doubt, fear, anger, and guilt.

This is one reason *Hand Guide to the Future* is being written, to encourage Christians to view this life from a heavenly perspective; understanding that in relation to eternity, our present existence, with all its ups and downs, pains and problems, is only a mere wink in time. Think of it this way: If eternity is an endless beach, our present life is only one grain of sand.

> For I reckon that the sufferings of this present time are not worthy to be compared with the glory which shall be revealed in us. (Romans 8:18)

In this life believers will suffer, but Scripture admonishes us to comprehend that the severity of our afflictions, trials, and tribulations is not worthy to be compared to "the *glory* which shall be revealed in us." Let's talk about this glory.

The Bible teaches that Christians will receive an eternal inheritance. We are heirs of God and joint-heirs with Christ. Jesus had a bodily resurrection; the dead in Christ will also have a bodily resurrection. Christ was raptured into heaven; we too will be raptured into heaven. Jesus was glorified with a new heavenly body; believers will also receive an everlasting, perfect body. We will be glorified together.

> The Spirit itself beareth witness with our spirit, that we are the children of God: And if children, then heirs; heirs of God, and joint-heirs with Christ; if so be that

Resurrection, Outtranslation, and Glorification

we suffer with him, that we may be also glorified together. (Romans 8:16–17)

Our temporal troubles, sicknesses, infirmities, and calamities are not worthy to be compared to the *glory* that will be revealed in us. And what is this glory? It is the eternal promise of God which includes a heavenly, state-of-the-art, glorified body.

Many precious believers are blind or have failing eyesight. One day God is going to give them the purest of vision—eyesight that would make an eagle jealous!

Others have difficulty walking or are confined to a bed or wheelchair. At the glorification, they'll be able to outrun the wind. "What in the world was that?" "Oh, that was just Brother Backstrom trying out those heaven-blessed legs; aren't they beautiful?" (Dick Backstrom is a close friend who has cerebral palsy.)

Over the years, some of God's people have cried "rivers of tears" over emotional distress. Beloved, the Balm of Gilead, the Mighty Healer, is going to erase the memory of all pain, suffering, and guilt. He will wipe away every tear.

> And God shall wipe away all tears from their eyes; and there shall be no more death, neither sorrow, nor crying, neither shall there be any more pain: for the former things are passed away. (Revelation 21:4)

First Corinthians 15 tells us that God created different bodies, both animate and inanimate. There are bodies terrestrial, sidereal, and celestial; there are heavenly and earthly bodies, each serving its own purpose.

> When you sow, you do not plant the body that will be, but just a seed, perhaps of wheat or of something else. But God gives it a body as he has determined, and to

> each kind of seed he gives its own body. All flesh is not the same: Men have one kind of flesh, animals have another, birds another and fish another. There are also heavenly bodies and there are earthly bodies; but the splendor of the heavenly bodies is one kind, and the splendor of the earthly bodies is another. The sun has one kind of splendor, the moon another and the stars another; and star differs from star in splendor. (1 Corinthians 15:37–41 NIV)

Christians are in a wonderfully unique position. They not only have the privilege of serving and loving God while in their earthly bodies, but they will also serve and love Him in their heavenly bodies, for "as we have borne the image of the earthly, we shall also bear the image of the heavenly" (1 Corinthians 15:49).

But what will these new, eternal bodies be like? Are you ready for a fantastic revelation straight from Scripture? Buckle up, for this is awesome! In John 17, Jesus prays for Himself, for His disciples, and then for all believers. Read carefully what He requests.

> I have glorified thee on the earth: I have finished the work which thou gavest me to do. And now, O Father, glorify thou me with thine own self with the glory which I had with thee before the world was. (John 17:4–5)

Jesus wasn't forced; He was willing to come out of eternity and give up the glory He had with the Father so humanity could be fully experienced. For thirty-three years Christ bore the image of the earthly, and because of His faithfulness to God, because of His sinlessness, He was able to offer the greatest love the world will ever see. He took the sins of humanity upon His

Resurrection, Outtranslation, and Glorification

shoulders, nailing the consequences to the cross. He died so that we might live.

> Your attitude should be the same as that of Christ Jesus: Who, being in very nature God, did not consider equality with God something to be grasped, but made himself nothing, taking the very nature of a servant, being made in human likeness. And being found in appearance as a man, he humbled himself and became obedient to death—even death on a cross! (Philippians 2:5–8 NIV)

In John chapter 17, Jesus knew He would soon be with the Father. He also knew He would be glorified with the glory that was His prior to the virgin birth. The Savior had borne the image of the earthly and would again bear the image of the heavenly. And part of the Lord's glorification included an eternal body—and we ask, "What does Christ's glorified body have to do with the one we receive?" This is so exciting; are you ready for this? Christ's glorified body has everything to do with ours, since *ours* will be like *His!* This is part of the Christian inheritance!

> But our citizenship is in heaven. And we eagerly await a Savior from there, the Lord Jesus Christ, who, by the power that enables him to bring everything under his control, *will transform our lowly bodies so that they will be like his glorious body.* (Philippians 3:20–21 NIV)

> And just as we have borne the likeness of the earthly man, so shall we bear the likeness of the man from heaven. (1 Corinthians 15:49 NIV)

> Dear friends, now we are children of God, and what we

will be has not yet been made known. But we know that when he [Jesus Christ] appears, we shall be like him, for we shall see him as he is. (1 John 3:2 NIV)

God has graciously given us this marvelous promise of glorification. It is something Christians can look forward to with great anticipation and expectation. This reality should inspire us to rejoice and thank the Lord for sharing such a precious revelation. However, we need to be cautious since some ministers have taken these verses completely out of context; erroneously surmising that since the believer's body will be like Jesus' body, Christians will somehow be deified—that they will become *gods*.

Nothing could be further from the truth. Our bodies will be like His in the sense of heavenly composition but not in divinity, power, or preeminence. Christ's eternal position as our Lord and Savior, as the second person of the Trinity, will forever be infinitely superior to ours. Any man-made comparison would fail to illustrate the vast distance.

A Glimpse at Christ's Glorified Body

Logically, if our heavenly bodies are going to be like Christ's, gaining information about their nature would have to be derived from looking at His. Unfortunately, there just isn't much data on the Savior's heavenly body. In fact, the church is not in complete agreement regarding when He was glorified. Some believe that Jesus was resurrected in a glorified state. Others assert the glorification was a long, drawn-out process beginning with the resurrection and ending in heaven. Still others claim Christ was not glorified until He sat down at the right hand of God and began His priestly ministry as our advocate and mediator.

Resurrection, Outtranslation, and Glorification

Is Scripture clear on this issue? I believe it is. First Corinthians 15 teaches that in relation to our new bodies, resurrection and glorification are synonyms.

> So also is the resurrection of the dead. It is sown in corruption; it is raised in incorruption: It is sown in dishonour; it is raised in glory: it is sown in weakness; it is raised in power: It is sown a natural body; it is raised a spiritual body. There is a natural body, and there is a spiritual body. (1 Corinthians 15:42–44)

Jesus is our pattern and example. His resurrection was the archetype, which means if the dead in Christ are resurrected in an immortal, glorified body, He too was resurrected fully glorified.

> Through him you believe in God, who raised him from the dead and glorified him, and so your faith and hope are in God. (1 Peter 1:21 NIV)

We will now examine what Scripture reveals about Christ's glorified body. Following His resurrection, Christ startled His disciples with an unexpected appearance, and they, at first, thought He was a ghost.

> He said to them, "Why are you troubled, and why do doubts rise in your minds? Look at my hands and my feet. It is I myself! Touch me and see; a ghost does not have flesh and bones, as you see I have." (Luke 24:38–39 NIV)

Christ was resurrected in a glorified, spiritual body—a body that by all intents and purposes looked human. It was both tangible and physical; it even bore the marks of the crucifixion. Albeit, it was not subject to the laws of nature as we will see in a moment. First Corinthians 15:50 says that flesh and blood cannot inherit the kingdom of God, which means the flesh and bones Jesus spoke of were not of earthly origin, although they seemed to be. To further prove He was not a ghost, Christ asked for something to eat.

> And when he had thus spoken, he shewed them his hands and his feet. And while they yet believed not for joy, and wondered, he said unto them, Have ye here any meat? And they gave him a piece of a broiled fish, and of an honeycomb. And he took it, and did eat before them. (Luke 24:40–43)

Christ appeared to be human. He spoke like a human, walked like a human, and ate like a human, but His body was spiritual. It had a dimension about it that made it capable of breaking our physical laws. (Please note that Jesus was also capable of breaking physical laws in His earthly body. He was after all, theanthropic (theanthropos)—the one and only God-man. However, we may also draw parallels between Christ's spiritual body following resurrection and the believer's glorified body following resurrection.)

> On the evening of that first day of the week, when the disciples were together, with the *doors locked* for fear of the Jews, Jesus came and stood among them and said, "Peace be with you!"...A week later his disciples were in the house again, and Thomas was with them. *Though the doors were locked,* Jesus came and stood among them and said, "Peace be with you!" (John 20:19, 26 NIV)

Doubting Thomas was able to physically handle Jesus, just as you and I can touch each other. Yet the Savior walked through a locked door as if it wasn't even there. Christ's glorified body could also change form, shape, and appearance.

Resurrection, Outtranslation, and Glorification

Afterward Jesus appeared in a different form to two of them while they were walking in the country. (Mark 16:12 NIV)

Subsequent to His resurrection, Jesus appeared to two disciples "in a different form." The Greek word for "form" is *morphe*, which is the root of our English word *morphosis*. *Morphe* means to "alter shape," to "change form, nature, or appearance." Mark's scanty observation concerning Jesus and the two disciples doesn't do justice to what actually transpired. Luke's account is much more detailed. He tells us these two Christian brothers were walking on the road to Emmaus, discussing what had happened to Christ. Jesus came up beside them, and His appearance was that of another person. They did not recognize who He was.

> Now that same day two of them were going to a village called Emmaus, about seven miles from Jerusalem. They were talking with each other about everything that had happened. As they talked and discussed these things with each other, Jesus himself came up and walked along with them; but they were kept from recognizing him. (Luke 24:13–16 NIV)

The words these men spoke reflected disappointment, ignorance, and a lack of faith. So Jesus chides them with the following:

> He said to them, "How foolish you are, and how slow of heart to believe all that the prophets have spoken! Did not the Christ have to suffer these things and then enter his glory?" (Luke 24:25–26 NIV)

Christ gave them a discourse on messianic prophecy (truth they should have already known), and because it was late in the day, they invited Him to spend the night. During dinner, the Savior allowed them to see who He really was—then disappeared.

> When he was at the table with them, he took bread, gave thanks, broke it and began to give it to them. Then their eyes were opened and they recognized him, and he disappeared from their sight. They asked each other, "Were not our hearts burning within us while he talked with us on the road and opened the Scriptures to us?" (Luke 24:30–32 NIV)

Jesus could not only go through material objects and change form, He was also able to disappear and reappear elsewhere. This indicates that His glorified body was capable of thought travel.

Our Heavenly Bodies

The Bible says that our spiritual bodies will be crafted in the likeness of Christ's body. He will "transform our lowly bodies so that they will be like his glorious body" (Philippians 3:21 NIV). What follows is a description of the Christian's glorified body. This description is based on both fact and conjecture. It contains elements that are 100 percent accurate, as well as elements that must be understood as theoretical:

1. Anatomically, the glorified body will have the appearance of a human. It will have a skeletal structure, flesh, human appendages, eyes, and so forth.

2. We learn in life that not all things are as they appear to be. The eternal body will look natural, but it will be spiritual. It will look human, but it will be heavenly. For "as we have borne the image of the earthly, we shall also bear the image of the heavenly" (1 Corinthians 15:49).

Resurrection, Outtranslation, and Glorification

3. The heavenly body will be able to deal with a material physical world on its terms, physical laws, but those terms shall not govern its abilities. This supernatural attribute will be great news for those of us who have a tendency of leaving keys in locked houses and cars. It will probably take time getting adjusted to making decisions, such as "Should I open the door, or just walk through it?"

4. The glorified body will have the same physical capabilities as an earthly human body, such as manipulative dexterity, or the ability to walk, run, or type. It may also have the exciting supernatural ability of thought travel. By thought travel, I don't mean it in the sense of Superman—a recognizable body speeding through the atmosphere, "Look, up in the sky! Is it a bird? Is it a plane?" No, it's just the author trying to explain that this would not be the heavenly body's method of thought travel. In Mark 16:12, the Greek word *morphe* was used to describe Christ's ability to change form and appearance. When Jesus disappeared in front of the two disciples and then reappeared elsewhere, He changed form and traveled by thought. What form would a heavenly body take in order to travel in this manner? Probably *light*. When Jesus came out of heaven and encircled Paul (then called Saul) on the Damascus Road, His form was that of light.

> As he neared Damascus on his journey, suddenly a light from heaven flashed around him. He fell to the ground and heard a voice say to him. "Saul, Saul, why do you persecute me?" "Who are you, Lord?" Saul asked. "I am Jesus, whom you are persecuting," he replied. (Acts 9:3–5 NIV)

5. This next characteristic of a heavenly body is something near and dear to most of our hearts: eating! Yes, in heaven we

will enjoy terrific food. Jesus ate in His glorified body. Following our resurrection, outtranslation, glorification, and the marriage of the Lamb, we will sit down to a scrumptious wedding feast.

> And he saith unto me, Write, Blessed are they which are called unto the marriage supper of the Lamb. And he saith unto me, These are the true sayings of God. (Revelation 19:9)

In New Jerusalem, on both sides of the river of life, will be trees of life bearing twelve varieties of fruit. Do you think they might be tasty?

> In the midst of the street of it, and on either side of the river, was there the tree of life, which bare twelve manner of fruits, and yielded her fruit every month: and the leaves of the tree were for the healing of the nations. (Revelation 22:2)

6. In the heavenly body the believer will experience perfect knowledge and perfect universal communication.

> Charity never faileth: but whether there be prophecies, they shall fail; whether there be tongues, they shall cease; whether there be knowledge, it shall vanish away. For we know in part, and we prophesy in part. But when that which is perfect is come, then that which is in part shall be done away. (1 Corinthians 13:8–10)

When "that which is perfect is come"—meaning the Christian's glorified state—"then that which is in part shall be done away." Believers do not see the complete picture from God's perspective. We are fallible. We make errors. We are certainly far from perfect. Knowledge and prophecy often fail because man has a fallen nature. But in the heavenly condition, the believer will have perfect knowledge, and "tongues" (foreign languages) shall cease. In heaven, Christians will experience perfect communication, both with each other—and with the Lord.

7. The spiritual body will be a heavenly state-of-the-art masterpiece. It will never get sick, never experience pain, never get too hot or cold, never go through emotional upheavals, and never mourn or weep. It will never have a broken bone or a cavity, and there will be no need for glasses or contacts. What am I saying? Continual emotional balance, continual health, joy unspeakable and full of glory!

8. Last but not least, the glorified body comes with an eternal "lifetime guarantee." Insured by, the "Mutual of Heaven," and their motto just happens to be, "You're in good hands with the Trinity!"

Brethren, when we contemplate the wonderful glory the Lord has prepared for His faithful children; when we meditate on His eternal promises, being heirs of God and joint-heirs with Christ; the world and its glory becomes ever so dim, and the trials we must endure for such a short time become unworthy "compared to the glory that will be revealed in us."

Chapter Five

THE CLOSING OF THIS AGE

Next on our journey through the future of mankind, we will take a look at the three millennial views and discover why this book, *Hand Guide to the Future*, is based on premillennialism. We then talk about crucial choices that every person will face when the Antichrist is revealed. Decisions that have eternal consequences: God or Satan? Antichrist or Jesus Christ? Heaven or hell? The chapter ends by closing out this present age. This will not be a pleasant subject; war never is. Because of man's rebellion against God, this dispensation concludes with the War of Armageddon.

The Closing of This Age

The Three Millennial Views

Within the framework of Christian orthodoxy are three differing millennial teachings: premillennialism, amillennialism, and postmillennialism. Although there has been a vigorous modern-day resurgence of postmillennialism through dominion theology, and amillennialism through "kingdom now" theology, premillennialism (or *chiliasm*) is the oldest, most scripturally consistent, literal position. This book has been written entirely from that view. While premillenarians have serious theological conflicts with amillennialism and postmillennialism, it is erroneous to label the adherents of either of these positions as heretical or cultic, simply on the basis of their millennial position.

The word *millennium* itself is not found in Scripture, but it refers to "a thousand years," which is mentioned in Revelation 20 six times. It also identifies with the Old Testament promises of a future kingdom of righteousness—the kingdom of Christ and the restoration of the Davidic kingdom. The word *millennium* is taken from two Latin words, *mille* meaning "thousand," and *annum* meaning "years." Thus a millennium is simply a thousand years.

Premillennialism

Premillennialism is based on the belief that Christ will return to earth at the end of this age, specifically at the end of the Great Tribulation. He will stop the War of Armageddon and institute a theocracy, a divine government of righteousness, which will last a thousand years. Christians (both Jew and Gentile) who return with Christ will be given positions of authority.

> They shall be priests of God and of Christ, and shall reign with him a thousand years. (Revelation 20:6)

Amillennialism

Amillennialists take a more allegorical view of eschatology. They deny a literal rapture of the church, as well as a future peaceful reign of Christ on earth. The amillenarian believes Satan was bound by Christ's atonement on the cross, and concerning the thousand years spoken of in Revelation 20, they are divided into two camps. Some believe saints are ruling with Christ in heaven; others believe that a "figurative" millennium is presently being played out on earth.

Since amillennialists deny a literal millennium, they generally accept the idea the thousand years spoken of in Revelation 20 is the time between Christ's First and Second Advent. Of course one doesn't have to be a nuclear scientist to figure out that almost two thousand years have passed since the Lord's First Coming. When the words *a thousand years* are not taken literally, they can be spiritualized to mean practically anything.

Let me quote a statement from Chapter 1: "While the Bible does contain allegories, hyperboles, and metaphors, a literal approach to interpretation should always be taken unless the context demands otherwise." When Peter wrote, "One day is with the Lord as a thousand years, and a thousand years as one day" (2 Peter 3:8), he was not setting a precedent for interpreting the phrase "a thousand years." He did not mean from that time forward it would be "open season" on interpretation—that *a thousand years* is a malleable phrase that can be shaped to fit any doctrinal point of view.

To an infinite, eternal God, time is basically irrelevant. In view of eternity, there is little significance to a day, as opposed to a thousand years. However, time is very important to us finite humans. Our whole existence centers around time: birth, aging, death, sleeping, appointments, events, school, and work. I know in my own life, it seems I've got to know the time throughout the entire day, and haven't we all been asked numerous times, "Pardon me, but do you have the time?"

It would be uncharacteristic for God to describe mankind's future in the Bible, giving us specific events and outlining in great detail the prophetic end-time scenario, then add something, *and shall reign with him a thousand years*, which no one could possibly grasp because it was written from an eternal, nonliteral, time perspective. This would make the study of certain prophetic events extremely confusing, and God is not the author of confusion.

Postmillennialism

Postmillennialism is the newest millennial position. This view did not truly differentiate itself from amillennialism until 1703, when Daniel Whitby's work, *Paraphrase and Commentary on the New Testament*, was published. Postmillennialism is based on the idea that Christ will not physically return to earth until the earth has been prepared for His arrival. According to the postmillennialist, this occurs at the end of the Millennium —the end of the thousand years described in Revelation 20.

The quintessential word for postmillennialism is *optimism*. To believe the world is progressively getting better, that Christian influence and values are steadily taking control, that Christ will return to a peaceful, Christianized world, is indeed the epitome of optimism.

Is the World Getting Better?

Are the postmillennialists right? How about the evolutionists or the new agers? Is the world really getting better?

In Matthew 24 and Luke 21, the disciples asked Jesus to give them signs pertaining to His Second Coming and the end of the world, "Tell us, when shall these things be? and what shall be the sign of thy coming, and of the end of the world?" (Matthew 24:3). Think about it: If postmillennial theology, evolutionary theories, and new age spirituality were correct in saying man is continually moving in positive directions, we would expect Jesus' answer to be full of positive statements—such as, "When I return, mankind will have advanced to a higher state of consciousness; his physical and spiritual evolution will have coalesced, creating a perfected man who is in harmony with all things. Yes, at my Second Coming humanity will have progressed to a state not capable of regressing to its former disruptive actions and attitudes. The world will be at peace—no more crime, violence, greed, or war."

However, different philosophies and theologies offering the illusionary hope of a perfect world (without the physical presence and assistance of Christ) are nothing more than pipe dreams. They fail to recognize the fallen nature of man which historically repeats the same mistakes over and over again. God's creation suffers the repercussions of rejecting His will, clearly revealed in His Word, the Bible.

When the disciples asked about end-time signs, Jesus did not paint a pretty picture. At the end of this age, humanity will be nowhere near utopia.

> And Jesus answered and said unto them, Take heed that no man deceive you. For many shall come in my name, saying, I am Christ; and shall deceive many. And ye shall hear of wars and rumours of wars: see that ye be not troubled: for all these things must come to pass, but the end is not yet. For nation shall rise against nation, and kingdom against kingdom: and there shall be famines, and pestilences, and earthquakes, in divers places. (Matthew 24:4–7)

The Closing of This Age

Verse 8 goes on to say, "All these are the beginning of sorrows." And Jesus said in verse 22 that if God did not shorten the days just prior to His return, "there should no flesh be saved." The encouraging news is that Scripture is abundantly clear that Christ will put an end to mankind's demise. He will establish an earthly kingdom of righteousness that will last a thousand years. We will discuss what is beyond this millennial period in Chapters 8 through 10.

Who Is Really Winning?

It would be nice if the dominionists and postmillennialists were correct in saying that Christ will return to a world in which His church has taken dominion—a Christianized "Garden of Eden" that has been prepared for His glory. Yes, it would be nice if an aspect of amillennialism were true—that public enemy number one, Satan and his demonic kingdom of darkness, are presently bound in chains, having no influence in world affairs or personal lives. But Satan is not bound in chains. He is the god of this world (2 Corinthians 4:4), and his end-time agenda is methodically coming to fruition. The devil's thousand-year prison term in the bottomless pit will not begin until his two hooligans, the Antichrist and the False Prophet, are cast into the lake of fire at the end of this age.

Contrary to the perception of even some premillennialists, Christianity is not winning the battle for the eternal souls of mankind. Praise God for churches, revivals, evangelism, and salvation. But the majority of the earth's population is being prepared to receive the Antichrist and the False Prophet, not Jesus Christ, "For by thy sorceries were *all nations* deceived" (Revelation 18:23).

Since its inception the United States has been called a

Christian nation. This would imply that most of our population is Christian. However, election after election we see men and women voted into office whose policies and beliefs are hostile to God, His Word, and His people. If citizens of a supposedly "Christian nation" desire leaders who promote anti-Christian policies—it is not difficult to comprehend how the world will eagerly accept both the Antichrist and the False Prophet.

Heaven and eternity will be filled with millions of joyous blood-bought believers, but that number pales in significance to those who, by free will choose the wide gate, the broad way, that leads to destruction. This means eternal hell (the lake of fire) will contain more souls than heaven, a fact militating against dominionism and postmillennialism.

> Enter ye in at the strait gate: for wide is the gate, and broad is the way, that leadeth to destruction, and many there be which go in thereat: Because strait is the gate, and narrow is the way, which leadeth unto life, and few there be that find it. (Matthew 7:13–14)

Folks, don't misunderstand what I'm saying. Christians are indeed winners in Christ, and we will eventually come out on top during the Millennium. But let's be honest and admit that if we, the church, were truly winning our society and world to the righteousness of God (to obedience to His Word), the beautiful fruits would be manifested everywhere! It would be reflected in lives that make Jesus Christ the focal point and God's Word the final authority. It would be evident in relationships and marriages, in the home and at school, on television, in movies, in politics, and in world affairs. Are we morally, ethically, and spiritually advancing—or are we declining? Statistics would suggest the latter! If anyone should doubt this, here's a little test. Read your daily newspaper from a biblical perspective and see if the news lines up with Philippians 4:8.

> Finally, brethren, whatsoever things are true, whatsoever things are honest, whatsoever things are just, whatsoever things are pure, whatsoever things are lovely, whatsoever things are of good report; if there be any virtue, and if there be any praise, think on these things. (Philippians 4:8)

Two White Horses Traveling in Opposite Directions

It's interesting: The time known as the Great Tribulation begins with a rider on a white horse going forth "conquering, and to conquer" (Revelation 6:2). And it ends with a rider on a white horse conquering the one who went forth conquering and to conquer, for "in righteousness he doth judge and make war" (Revelation 19:11).

It is not surprising that the Antichrist—the first rider of the "four horsemen of the apocalypse"—is riding an allegorical white horse in Revelation 6, as is Jesus Christ in Revelation 19. *Allegorical* simply means that "Mr. 666" is not going to be riding a literal white horse during his rise to power nor during the Great Tribulation.

Jesus Christ is the righteousness of God—a Light unto a darkened world, the only hope this planet has. His return on a figurative white horse represents these qualities. The Antichrist's white horse signifies he will come on the scene exuding exemplary qualities: The old white hat, sunshine reflecting off the front tooth kind of guy.

What the Bible reveals is that there will be two white horses traveling in opposite directions. One leads to heaven; the other leads to hell. At the end of this present age, they will meet for a showdown at the "Armageddon Corral." The Antichrist will bite the dust even before his weapon clears his holster.

Humanity Must Choose

Just as Adolf Hitler was able to mesmerize a whole nation with anti-God, anti-Semitic rhetoric, the world will be enthralled with the influential, charismatic white horse rider of Revelation 6, "And there was given unto him a mouth speaking great things and blasphemies" (Revelation 13:5).

Unlike Hitler's dynamic hostility, the Antichrist will speak peaceful words of demonic seduction to a world whose ears and hearts have been closed to the gospel of Christ. He will captivate the minds of those who have no intention of reading and heeding God's prophetic words of warning.

The Bible warns: Do not follow the Antichrist! But the world will enthusiastically follow the Antichrist (Revelation 13:3–7).

The Bible warns: Do not be fooled by the miracle-working False Prophet! But the world will be captivated by his benevolence and his supernatural power (Revelation 13:13–14).

The Bible warns: Do not take the mark of the beast! But this satanic identification mark will be eagerly accepted (Revelation 13:16–17; 14:9–11).

The Bible warns: Listen to the two witnesses! They will tell you how to obtain victory—how to escape eternal damnation! But the world will despise the witnesses and celebrate their death (Revelation 11:9–10).

The Bible warns: The judgments poured out during the Great Tribulation through the seals, trumpets, and vials are signs telling people to repent! But for the most part, the world will refuse to repent (Revelation 9:20–21; 16:9; 16:11).

> Blessed is he that readeth, and they that hear the words of this prophecy, and keep those things which are written therein: for the time is at hand (Revelation 1:3).

How sad it is. People will pay horrendous consequences for listening to the wrong message, for willfully accepting the Antichrist rather than redemption through Jesus Christ, for choosing the god of this world instead of the God of the Bible, and for yielding themselves to every idea and philosophy that exalts itself above God's will and His Word.

Christians serve a God of love. But this love is not defined in a giggly, gooey–sweet manner (God is in everything, and He loves everyone; no one will go to hell because God is love). But God doesn't love sin and rebellion. He doesn't love Satan, demons, the Antichrist, or the False Prophet. And anyone who identifies with their end–time harlot system by taking the mark of the beast will get a taste of God's "tough love." They will experience eternal judgment before His Great White Throne.

> And whosoever was not found written in the book of life was cast into the lake of fire. (Revelation 20:15)

A Call to Armageddon

To say the Antichrist will have the gift of gab is a gross understatement. With feigned lips and a devious heart, this demigod will seduce the nations of the world into a socioeconomic relationship. He will use the allure of wealth (Revelation 18:3) and a seemingly foolproof population control system (Revelation 13:16–17). The Antichrist's oratorical excellence will be further exhibited at the end of this age when he, through the power of Satan and with the assistance of his comrade the False Prophet, calls the world to Armageddon. This will be the final event of the Great Tribulation.

> And I saw three unclean spirits like frogs come out of the mouth of the dragon [Satan], and out of the mouth of the beast [the Antichrist], and out of the mouth of the false prophet. For they are the spirits of devils, working miracles, which go forth unto the kings of the earth and of the whole world, to gather them to the battle of that great day of God Almighty...And he gathered them together into a place called in the Hebrew tongue Armageddon. (Revelation 16:13–14, 16)

The Hebrew word *Armageddon* is derived from the word *Har-Megiddo*, which means "mountain or hill of Megiddo." Megiddo is an ancient town located approximately sixty miles north of Jerusalem. Megiddo overlooks the Plain of Megiddo, which has a rather bloody history, including the following events:

- The battle of Barak against the Canaanites (Judges 4:15–16).
- The conflict of Gideon and the Midianites (Judges 7).
- Saul's death in the battle against the Philistines (1 Samuel 31).
- Josiah's defeat by Pharaoh-nechoh, which resulted in Judah losing its freedom to Egypt (2 Kings 23:29–30).
- The English general Edmund Allenby's defeat by the Turkish army in World War I.

The Plain of Megiddo is where the great conflagration of the world's militaries will gather for the War of Armageddon.

Revelation 16 says that the Euphrates River will be dried up so the "kings of the east" can cross with no difficulty (Revelation 16:12). It has been reported the Turkish people are capable of shutting off the flow of the Euphrates River at a moment's notice.

Some believe the war of Ezekiel 38—39 is synonymous with the War of Armageddon. Others (myself included) believe these are two different wars. Exactly who will participate in the War of Armageddon is open for debate. However, we can be absolutely certain of the following:

- There will be a War of Armageddon.
- Many nations will be involved, including Israel.
- It will be fought on the Plain of Megiddo, probably also in the valley of Jezreel, the Jordan Valley, and the valley of Jehoshaphat (Joel 3:2–12).
- It will be the bloodiest war in history.
- The Antichrist will be its instigator.
- Jesus Christ will return to earth and inflict terminal punishment on those involved.

The End of This Age

As the world's military forces are waging war on the Plain of Megiddo, in heaven a victorious church will be preparing to return to earth. We have seen that the Great Tribulation begins with the Antichrist riding on an allegorical white horse (Revelation 6:2) and ends with Jesus Christ returning on a figurative white horse (Revelation 19:11). Revelation 19:14 reveals the Christian armies in heaven will be riding on similar white horses. These allegorical white horses and the clean, white linen signify that the church is one with the Savior and that God's people are clothed in Christ's righteousness—ready, willing, and able to carry out His will.

> And the armies which were in heaven followed him upon white horses, clothed in fine linen, white and clean. (Revelation 19:14)

Revelation 19:13 says, "And he [Jesus Christ] was clothed with a vesture dipped in blood." This is the fulfillment of an Old Testament prophecy found in Isaiah 63:1–4. This unique prophecy appears as a sequence of questions and answers between Israel and God.

> Israel: Who is this that cometh from Edom, with dyed garments from Bozrah? this that is glorious in his apparel, travelling in the greatness of his strength?
> The Lord: I that speak in righteousness, mighty to save.
> Israel: Wherefore art thou red in thine apparel, and thy garments like him that treadeth in winefat?
> The Lord: I have trodden the winepress alone; and of the people there was none with me: for I will tread them in mine anger, and trample them in my fury; and their blood shall be sprinkled upon my garments, and I will stain all my raiment. For the day of vengeance is in mine heart, and the year of my redeemed is come.

Like a man whose clothes become stained from trampling grapes, Christ will trample the armies of Armageddon, splattering their rebellious blood upon His garments. At His First Coming, Christ was a meek humble man, and although more than twelve legions of angels could have been summoned at any given time (Matthew 26:53), He allowed Himself to be abused, eventually dying on the cross so Scripture could be

The Closing of This Age

fulfilled (Matthew 26:54). He was obedient to His Father from birth to death, "And being found in fashion as a man, he humbled himself, and became obedient unto death, even the death of the cross" (Philippians 2:8).

Christ's Second Coming will be an entirely different story. He is not coming to humbly submit Himself to the godless dictates of man; nor will He allow Himself to be beaten and dragged before pagan ad hoc courts. Jesus will never again be judged by any man, for He is the judge and is returning as Lord of lords and King of kings. Our Savior's Second Advent will be one of righteous indignation—of holy vengeance upon those who have rejected the true Christ and accepted the Antichrist. Those who blasphemed God's holy name, rebelled against His Word, and persecuted and killed His beloved children.

> And when he had opened the fifth seal, I saw under the altar the souls of them that were slain for the word of God, and for the testimony which they held: And they cried with a loud voice, saying, How long, O Lord, holy and true, dost thou not judge and avenge our blood on them that dwell on the earth? And white robes were given unto every one of them; and it was said unto them, that they should rest yet for a little season, until their fellowservants also and their brethren, that should be killed as they were, should be fulfilled. (Revelation 6:9–11)

In Revelation 19, Jesus is said to possess a sword—a sword He uses to defeat the forces at Armageddon. Admittedly, I would love to see an action-packed motion picture where the Lord's army is portrayed as a heavenly host of sword-wielding swashbucklers, ready to square off with the Antichrist's armies! It would be good versus evil—light versus darkness—and of course, the Lord's army would win with only minor casualties. That would make an exciting movie, but one far to the left of reality and accuracy. The sword spoken of in Revelation 19 proceeds out of the mouth of Jesus, not from a sheath (Revelation 19:15, 21).

Hebrews 4:12 tells us that the Word of God is sharper than any two-edged sword. The only weapon Christ will need on the battlefield of Armageddon is His Word of judgment.

At the Second Advent, when the church returns to earth with Jesus Christ, the Antichrist will order the armies of the world to attack this huge, rather strange-looking group that has suddenly appeared out of nowhere.

> And I saw the beast, and the kings of the earth, and their armies, gathered together to make war against him that sat on the horse, and against his army. (Revelation 19:19)

During the War of Armageddon, Jesus will first speak judgment against the Antichrist and the False Prophet. One moment they'll be on the sidelines shouting out commands; the next they'll find themselves in the lake of fire, scratching their heads and wondering what happened (Revelation 19:20). The Lord will then speak judgment against all the troops involved in the battle, and in a split second they become carrion for scavenger birds.

> And the remnant were slain with the sword of him that sat upon the horse, which sword proceeded out of his mouth: and all the fowls were filled with their flesh. (Revelation 19:21)

Observing this massive extermination will not be pleasant; however, two thousand years ago God prophesied, He warned

The Closing of This Age

that man's rebellion would cause this age to go out with a bang, and so it shall! At the end of the age, the focus of the church will not be on those who perished throughout the Great Tribulation, or the War of Armageddon. Instead, the saints will rejoice in the peace that Jesus Christ brings to the entire world. It will be a time of restoration in which the church will take an active role. It will be the dawning of a new era called the Millennium.

Chapter Six

MILLENNIAL TRANSITION

Before we put on our hip boots and wade into the time known as the Millennium, this chapter will address some peripheral subjects.

We will begin by bringing out a fact you may find interesting concerning the Antichrist and the False Prophet.

No White Throne Judgment for These Two!

Chapter 5 ended with a look at what Scripture reveals about the closing of our present age. We have seen that when Jesus and the saints return to earth, the Lord's first action will be to cast both the Antichrist and the False Prophet into eternal hell (the lake of fire). Take a moment to ponder the following questions:

1. Are the Antichrist and the False Prophet simply two wicked, deceived individuals working for Satan—or does it go beyond that?

2. Will they be judged with the rest of unsaved humanity at the Great White Throne Judgment?

Before answering, it is important to understand when the Bible mentions hell, it is not always referring to the same location. "Hell," translated from the Greek word *Hades*, or the Hebrew word *Sheol*—is not the same place as "hell," translated from the Greek word *Gehenna* (also called the lake of fire).

Hell (Hades) is the spirit prison where the unsaved dead are kept until the time of God's White Throne Judgment, "The Lord knoweth how to deliver the godly out of temptation, and to *reserve the unjust unto the day of judgment to be punished*" (2 Peter 2:9). Hell (Gehenna), or the lake of fire, is eternal hell. It is the place God originally designed for Satan and demons.

> Then shall he say also unto them on the left hand, Depart from me, ye cursed, into everlasting fire, prepared for the devil and his angels. (Matthew 25:41)

At the end of the Millennium, God will resurrect the souls out of "hell" Hades, judge them before His Great White Throne, then cast them into "hell" Gehenna—which is the lake of fire.

> And death and hell were cast into the lake of fire. This is the second death. (Revelation 20:14)

If there were only one hell, Revelation 20:14 would not make much sense, because it literally says "hell" will be cast into "hell." How can something be cast into itself? Following the

White Throne Judgment, the souls imprisoned in hell (Hades) will be cast into hell (Gehenna), which is eternal hell, also referred to as the lake of fire.

Besides spending eternity in hell, the unregenerate have one thing in common. They will all be present at the White Throne Judgment. No matter how vile or wicked, the unredeemed deserve to stand before God, where the books that contain the "documents" of people's entire lives will be opened and examined. They will see all the opportunities God graciously gave them to be saved. They will see how the Holy Spirit worked on their behalf without violating their free will. God will pass judgment, but it is man who condemns himself.

> But I say unto you, That every idle word that men shall speak, they shall give account thereof in the day of judgment. For by thy words thou shalt be justified, and by thy words thou shalt be condemned. (Matthew 12:36–37)

> He that believeth on him is not condemned: but he that believeth not is condemned already, because he hath not believed in the name of the only begotten Son of God. (John 3:18)

The Adolf Hitlers of this world will be at the White Throne Judgment, as will unrepentant mass murderers and satanists. Every unsaved human being throughout all of history deserves to face God in judgment prior to entering eternal hell—that is, except two! The Antichrist and the False Prophet! These two will be thrown directly into Gehenna at the beginning of the Millennium (Revelation 19:20). The Antichrist and the False Prophet will be the first occupants of eternal hell.

During the millennial reign of Christ, Satan will be bound

Millennial Transition

in the bottomless pit, so his kingdom of darkness doesn't enter Gehenna until one thousand years following the Antichrist and the False Prophet. We know Satan will not be judged at the White Throne Judgment; we know demons will not be judged there. But why not the Antichrist and the False Prophet? After all, won't they be human? They certainly will appear to be. So how come they don't deserve what even the vilest person on earth deserves? Because they will be on the same wavelength as Satan and demon spirits who have already been judged and sentenced.

When Lucifer and one-third of the angels in heaven rebelled against God and were expelled from their heavenly estate, their names were changed to words that describe their fallen nature. For example: Satan means "adversary," devil means "accuser and slanderer," Beelzebub means "lord of dung," and demons denote "evil spirits."

Although the Antichrist will have a real name, the Bible refers to him with names that reflect his true nature, such as: the beast, "a dangerous animal—venomous," man of lawlessness, "he violates the divine laws of God," son of perdition, "he is the son of destruction; the son of evil; the son of hell," and the Antichrist, "he is against Christ, and offers himself as a Christ."

The False Prophet will also have a regular name, but because he is in league with Satan and the Antichrist, Scripture refuses to refer to him with a dignified name. It instead calls him: False Prophet, "a prophet of Satan who cleverly masquerades as a prophet of God." He is also referred to by one of the Antichrist names, another beast, "a venomous, dangerous animal."

When Lucifer and the angels he deceived turned against God, they were not only cast out of heaven, but also cast out of God's will. Neither would they seek forgiveness nor receive it.

The same is true for the Antichrist and the False Prophet. They know who God is, they know who Jesus Christ is, and they know how powerful the Holy Spirit is. Yet, they despise the Holy Trinity because they are part of the "unholy Trinity," which is comprised of the father "Satan," the son "the Antichrist," and the unholy spirit "the False Prophet."

The preincarnate Christ came out of eternity. He was born and raised for a single purpose. Likewise, the destinies and eternal judgments of the Antichrist and the False Prophet could quite possibly have been determined even before their birth. They will be abnormal, supernaturally powered, demonic people—human, yes, but completely possessed! And so it stands to reason that there will be "no White Throne Judgment for these two!"

> And the dragon [Satan] gave him [the Antichrist] his power, and his seat, and great authority. (Revelation 13:2b)

Satan Bound for a Thousand Years

In Revelation 12, a war takes place in heaven (sidereal or atmospheric heaven) between the archangel Michael and his army, and Satan's kingdom of darkness. This war occurs three and one-half years before the end of this age. It results in Satan losing his "supersonic" mobility—his ability to travel through the lower two heavens. Satan is also stripped of the privilege of approaching God in order to accuse Christians of their sins. This reduction of power infuriates the devil and is a sign that his time is just about up.

> And I heard a loud voice saying in heaven, Now is come salvation, and strength, and the kingdom of our God, and the power of his Christ: for the accuser of our

Millennial Transition

> brethren is cast down, which accused them before our God day and night...Therefore rejoice, ye heavens, and ye that dwell in them. Woe to the inhabitant of the earth and of the sea! for the devil is come down unto you, having great wrath, because he knoweth that he hath but a short time. (Revelation 12:10, 12)

After wreaking havoc on earth for three and one-half years through the Antichrist and the False Prophet, Satan's reign—his "unholy Trinity"—comes to a screeching halt. In Revelation 9, we saw that an angel was given the key to the bottomless pit (not to be confused with Hades or Gehenna), which was opened to release demonic locusts. In all of Bible prophecy, this was the first time the abyss was ever opened. The first opening was to let evil out; the second opening will be to put the evil one in!

> And I saw an angel come down from heaven, having the key of the bottomless pit and a great chain in his hand. And he laid hold on the dragon, that old serpent, which is the Devil, and Satan, and bound him a thousand years, And cast him into the bottomless pit, and shut him up, and set a seal upon him, that he should deceive the nations no more, till the thousand years should be fulfilled: and after that he must be loosed a little season. (Revelation 20:1–3)

What a glorious event this will be! God's nemesis—the father of lies, the deceiver of nations, and the perverter of souls—will be bound for a thousand years. An angel (probably Michael) will grab ole slough-foot, wrapping him in restraints the great Houdini couldn't escape from. Then as an added measure of security, God's seal of bondage is stamped upon him. Maximum security, to the max!

I don't believe we will truly comprehend the extent of Satan's oppressive spiritual power until it has been eliminated from the world.

A Great Reduction in The World's Population

Matthew 24:22 says that if God did not shorten the Great Tribulation, no one would survive, "And except those days should be shortened, there should no flesh be saved." And in Isaiah 24, the Lord said following His burning judgments there would be few men left on earth.

> Therefore hath the curse devoured the earth, and they that dwell therein are desolate: therefore the inhabitants of the earth are burned, and few men left. (Isaiah 24:6)

Compared with the world's huge population prior to the Great Tribulation, there will be few men left at its conclusion. Of course, it would be impossible to calculate the exact number that will survive this period, but we can look at a few Scriptures, jostle some figures, and come up with a "guesstimate." If the Great Tribulation were to begin today, we would be dealing with a world population of approximately 5.4 billion people (5,420,000,000). Let's quickly take a look at some judgments that cause death:

- Third trumpet, Revelation 8:11, "many men died of the waters, because they were made bitter."
- Sixth trumpet, Revelation 9:15, "to slay the third part of men;" Revelation 9:18, "by these three was the third part of men killed."
- Revelation 11:13, "in the earthquake were slain of men seven thousand."
- Revelation 19:21, "and the remnant were slain with the sword of him that sat upon the horse."

Millennial Transition

The largest religion in the world is Christianity, with an estimated membership of one billion people. If a billion Christians are raptured from the earth, the world's population would be reduced to 4.4 billion (4,420,000,000). The sixth trumpet judgment will slay one-third of the population, reducing the number of people to approximately 2,946,666,667. Seven thousand will be killed in the earthquake described in Revelation 11:13. This leaves 2,946,658,667 people.

Since Scripture does not give us the figures, the rest of our "guesstimate" is sheer speculation. The War of Armageddon will take more lives than any previous war—nuclear weapons will likely be used. Then we have the "many men" killed because of poisoned water, and all the intangible deaths due to other judgments. Two billion is probably a fair guess, and if it is within radar range, it means the earth would have less than a billion people entering the Millennium from a Great Tribulation beginning population of 5.4 billion.

Taking into consideration those raptured alive and the dead in Christ taken in the first resurrection, the number of glorified saints on earth during the beginning of the Millennium will far exceed the number of those who come out of the Great Tribulation.

During the time of God's wrath, Israel's judgment will be quite severe. Only a third of its population will survive. This means if the Great Tribulation were to happen today, Israel's present population of 4.7 million (4,748,059) would be reduced to 1.5 million (1,582,687). The good news is all of the Jewish survivors will accept Jesus Christ as their Messiah, as their Lord and Savior. This will be the fulfillment of Romans 11:26: "And so all Israel shall be saved."

And it shall come to pass, that in all the land, saith the

Lord, two parts therein shall be cut off and die; but the third shall be left therein. And I will bring the third part through the fire, and will refine them as silver is refined, and will try them as gold is tried: they shall call on my name, and I will hear them: I will say, It is my people: and they shall say, The Lord is my God. (Zechariah 13:8–9)

Wilt Thou Restore the Kingdom to Israel?

On the day Jesus was to ascend into heaven riding on the clouds of glory, the disciples came to Him asking, "Lord, wilt thou at this time restore again the kingdom to Israel?" (Acts 1:6). This was an issue near and dear to their hearts because after all, they were Jewish and understood the Old Testament promises to restore the kingdom as it was during the reign of David and Solomon.

"In that day I will restore David's fallen tent. I will repair its broken places, restore its ruins, and build it as it used to be...I will plant Israel in their own land, never again to be uprooted from the land I have given them." says the Lord your God. (Amos 9:11, 15 NIV)

Palestine was under the aegis of Rome, and the disciples were hoping Jesus would do one last thing before leaving earth, *restore again the kingdom to Israel.* Christ told them not to worry about Israel's restoration; that God would bring this about in His own time, "It is not for you to know the times or the seasons, which the Father hath put in his own power" (Acts 1:7). Unbeknownst to the disciples, many years and many events would pass before the Davidic kingdom would be restored:

Millennial Transition

1. The destruction of Jerusalem and Herod's Temple by the Roman army under Titus in A.D. 70.
2. The dispersion of the Jews.
3. The regathering of Jews in 1948, when Israel was officially declared a nation.
4. Wars, rumors of wars, famines, pestilences, earthquakes in many places, false christs and false prophets, and the preaching of the gospel to all the world (Matthew 24:6–7, 14, 24).
5. The rise of the Antichrist, the False Prophet, the ten kings, new world order, the harlot church, and the mark of the beast (Revelation 13 and 17).
6. The ministry of the 144,000 Christian Jews (Revelation 7:3–8).
7. The seven-year covenant between the Antichrist and Israel (Daniel 9:27).
8. The abomination of desolation (Daniel 9:27; Matthew 24:15; 2 Thessalonians 2:4).
9. The Great Tribulation (seen in the seven seals, trumpets, and vials of Revelation).
10. The first resurrection and the rapture of the church, which occurs somewhere in this outline depending on which rapture position (pretribulation, midtribulation, or posttribulation) is correct (1 Thessalonians 4:13–17).
11. The Bema Seat Judgment (Romans 14:10–12).
12. God's protection of one-third of Israeli Jews during the Great Tribulation (Revelation 12:14). Remember, Zechariah 13:8–9 reveals that two-thirds of the Jewish population will be killed during God's fiery judgments.
13. The ministry of the two witnesses (Revelation 11:3–12).

14. The marriage of the Lamb and the wedding feast (Revelation 19:7–9).
15. The War of Armageddon (Revelation 16:12–16; 19:19).
16. Christ's return with His saints, which includes the Lord ending the War of Armageddon and slaying its combatants (Revelation 19:11–21).
17. The casting of the Antichrist and the False Prophet into the lake of fire (Revelation 19:20).
18. The binding of Satan into the bottomless pit for a thousand years (Revelation 20:1–3).

This is not an exhaustive list, but can you imagine the reaction of the disciples if Jesus had laid this list on them when they asked (around two thousand years ago) "Wilt thou at this time restore again the kingdom to Israel?" *Say what? You've got to be kidding!*

The apostles have had to wait quite awhile. However, with the groundwork laid for the revealing of the Antichrist, his world system, and the harlot church, we must be near the fulfillment of all the items in this list. What a fabulous future is in store for both the Jew and the Gentile!

Thy Kingdom Come, Thy Will Be Done

The prayer that is most often prayed from Scripture is the Lord's Prayer, found in Matthew 6:9–13. With hearts full of love and reverence, the church joyfully says, "Thy kingdom come. Thy will be done in earth, as it is in heaven" (Matthew 6:10). Then we look out at a world filled with sin, rebellion, great perplexities, and confusion, knowing fully well that God's will is *not* being carried out here as it is in heaven.

Matthew 6:10 is a prophetic verse that points to the day

Millennial Transition

when the righteous laws of heaven will be strictly enforced on earth. This can never be accomplished through man's noble efforts, no matter how much energy, time, and money is spent. The earth is under a curse; man has a fallen nature; Satan is the god of this world; the Antichrist and the False Prophet are about to emerge; and the Great Tribulation is coming.

The apostle Paul admonishes the church to "fight the good fight of faith" (1 Timothy 6:12) and to "have no fellowship with the unfruitful works of darkness, but rather reprove them" (Ephesians 5:11). The light of the Lord needs to shine through His church. It needs to reach a darkened world with a spirit of love, boldness, and truth.

That said, the church is in no position, it has no power, to bring about "heaven on earth." Oh, we can and certainly do win significant battles; praise God for His faithful servants! But the war for world dominance and universal righteousness cannot be won by anyone except Jesus Christ. He and He alone has the power to thwart Satan's destructive end-time agenda and fulfill our prayer, "Thy kingdom come. Thy will be done in earth, as it is in heaven" (Matthew 6:10).

Chapter Seven

THE MILLENNIUM

A Millennium of Ease?

At the end of this age (the beginning of the Millennium), the earth will have been devastated and humanity decimated. The War of Armageddon will have taken its toll.

And the great city was divided into three parts, and the cities of the nations fell...(Revelation 16:19a)

Earthquakes and other judgments will have destroyed cities, homes, hospitals, schools, factories, power and water systems.

The Millennium

Most of the fresh water supply will have been contaminated; the oceans and seas polluted (Revelation 8:8–11; 16:3–6).

The Millennium is often portrayed as a Sunday stroll through the park, a picnic at Disneyland—a time when Christians lazily kick back on hammocks, sipping ice-cold lemonade, catching a few rays. When Isaiah spoke of the wolf living with the lamb, the leopard lying down with the goat, the lion eating hay like an ox, and children playing around with deadly snakes (Isaiah 11:6–8), he was metaphorically speaking of a time of peace, a time when the destructive weapons of war will be turned into productive implements of peace.

> And they shall beat their swords into plowshares, and their spears into pruninghooks: nation shall not lift up a sword against nation, neither shall they learn war anymore. (Micah 4:3b)

The truth is, during the Millennium the church, along with the rest of humanity, will be busier than "twelve bees at apple blossom time," helping Jesus Christ restore the earth. It will involve hard work and take many years to organize and rebuild. Fortunately, we will have a thousand years in which to do it!

Who Will Be King of Israel?

Many Old Testament passages speak of David as the king of Israel during the Millennium, and many speak of Christ as king. The fact that no verses mention them together (e.g., David and the Messiah shall reign as one) has brought about various conclusions. Jewish scholars tend to say that the passages referring to Christ are actually identifying David, while some in Christendom believe when David is mentioned as Israel's potentate, the Scriptures are actually talking about the greater David—Jesus Christ.

> And David my servant shall be king over them; and they all shall have one shepherd: they shall also walk in my judgments, and observe my statutes, and do them. And they shall dwell in the land that I have given unto Jacob my servant, wherein your fathers have dwelt; and they shall dwell therein, even they, and their children, and their children's children for ever: and my servant David shall be their prince for ever. (Ezekiel 37:24–25)

Identifying David as Jesus or Jesus as David is generally done to force Scripture into fitting a particular belief system. I see no valid reason for doing this except in those instances when the context demands such an interpretation. During the thousand-year reign of Christ, there will be various leadership positions. Jesus will be the supreme authority over every nation and tongue. David will be reinstated as ruler over his long-lost kingdom. The Davidic kingdom will be restored. Regarding the Jews, David will share a kind of co-regency with Christ. To be certain, David will carry out the will of his Lord and Savior, Jesus Christ.

Millennial Government

The governmental structure during the Millennium is quite fascinating. The Bible is clear that Jesus Christ will return to earth as Lord of lords and King of kings. He will be anointed president over the entire world. Israel will become the capital nation, Jerusalem its capital city, and the temple in Jerusalem will be its capitol building. Christ's theocratic government will be the fulfillment of many biblical prophecies, including this marvelous passage in Isaiah 9:

The Millennium

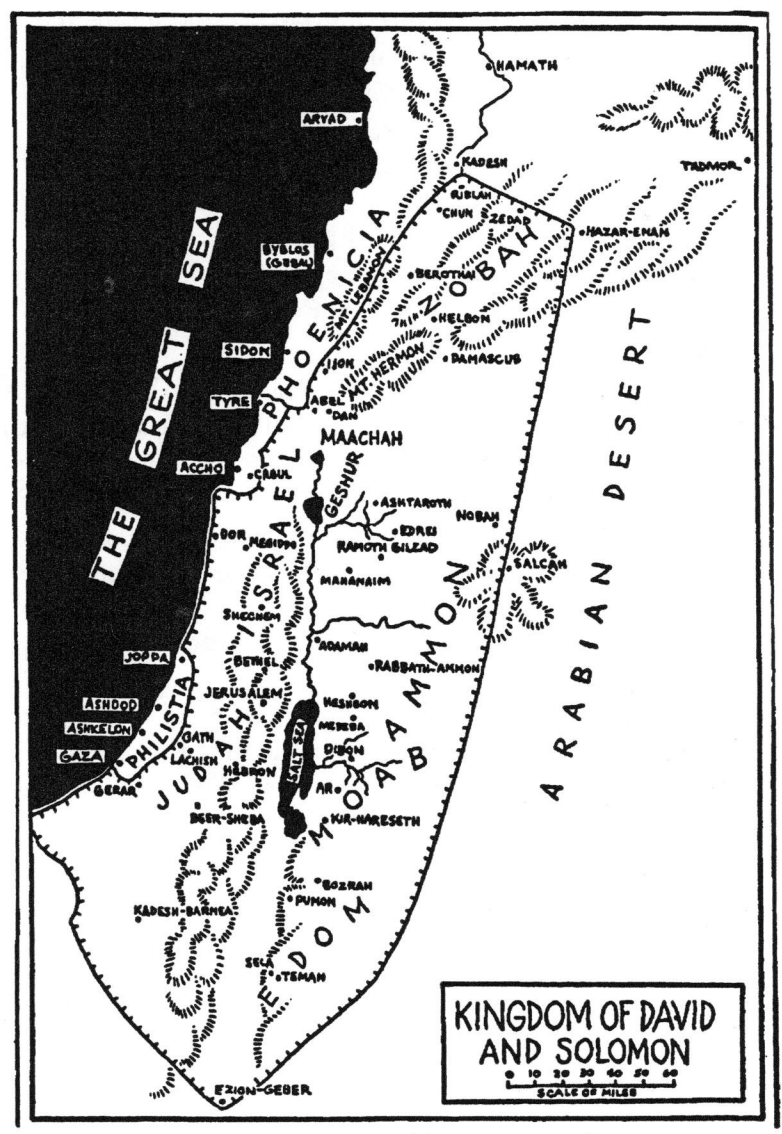

From *Unger's Bible Dictionary*.[1]

For unto us a child is born, unto us a son is given: and the government shall be upon his shoulder: and his name shall be called Wonderful, Counsellor, The mighty God, The everlasting Father, The Prince of Peace. Of the increase of his government and peace there shall be no end, upon the throne of David, and upon his kingdom, to order it, and to establish it with judgment and with justice from henceforth even for ever. The zeal of the Lord of hosts will perform this. (Isaiah 9:6–7)

Christ will rule the world from Jerusalem; His headquarters will be in the Millennial Temple. The Millennium begins with the Lord meting out different levels of authority and leadership. David will be given the great honor of regaining his rulership over Israel; however, it will not be tiny, present-day Israel, but Israel as it was during his former reign (see map on page 129).

Restoration of the Davidic Kingdom

You will recall that in Acts 1:6 the disciples asked Jesus, "Wilt thou at this time restore again the kingdom to Israel?" The kingdom they spoke of was the one so often prophesied in the Old Testament—the restored Davidic kingdom.

Afterward shall the children of Israel return, and seek the Lord their God, and David their king; and shall fear the Lord and his goodness in the latter days. (Hosea 3:5)

Incline your ear, and come unto me: hear, and your soul shall live; and I will make an everlasting covenant with you, even the sure mercies of David. Behold, I have given him for a witness to the people, a leader and commander to the people. (Isaiah 55:3–5)

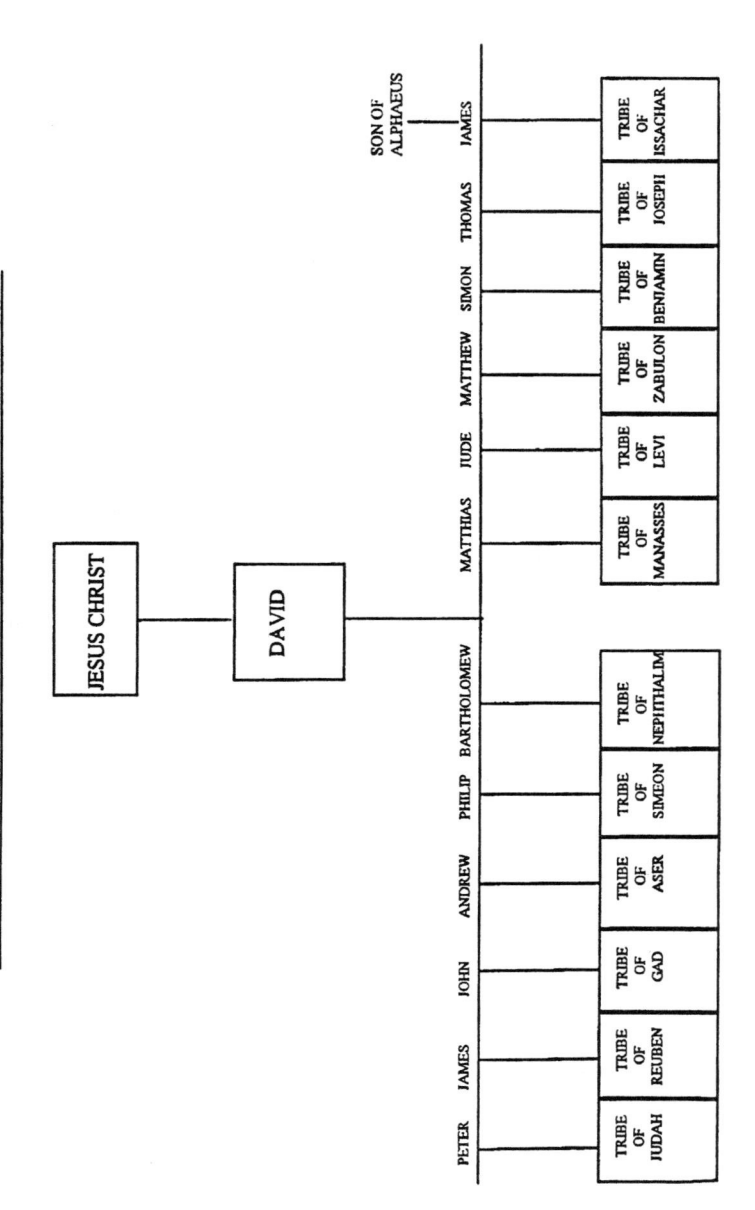

The Millennium

DAVIDIC KINGDOM GOVERNMENTAL STRUCTURE

JESUS CHRIST — DAVID

PETER	TRIBE OF JUDAH
JAMES	TRIBE OF REUBEN
JOHN	TRIBE OF GAD
ANDREW	TRIBE OF ASER
PHILIP	TRIBE OF SIMEON
BARTHOLOMEW	TRIBE OF NEPHTHALIM
MATTHIAS	TRIBE OF MANASSES
JUDE	TRIBE OF LEVI
MATTHEW	TRIBE OF ZABULON
SIMON	TRIBE OF BENJAMIN
THOMAS	TRIBE OF JOSEPH
JAMES (SON OF ALPHAEUS)	TRIBE OF ISSACHAR

131

Under Christ, David will be commander in chief over Israel. His political cabinet will consist of the twelve apostles: Peter, James, John, Andrew, Philip, Thomas, Bartholomew, Matthew, James (son of Alphaeus), Simon, Jude, and Matthias. These twelve apostles will judge (rule over) the twelve tribes of Israel.

> And Jesus said unto them, Verily I say unto you, That ye which have followed me, in the regeneration when the Son of man shall sit in the throne of his glory, ye also shall sit upon twelve thrones, judging the twelve tribes of Israel. (Matthew 19:28)

Every Jewish person is a descendant of one of the twelve tribes of Israel. In Revelation 7, we see that twelve thousand people from each of these tribes will be ministers of Christ during the Great Tribulation (Revelation 7:3–8). It will be interesting to learn whether each apostle is a descendant of the particular tribe he is to govern. The diagram on page 131 shows the governmental structure of the future Davidic kingdom. Of course, we cannot accurately match each apostle with a tribe, so the placement is not to be taken literally.

The Governmental Structure of the Davidic Kingdom

As Israel grows in population during the Millennium, the responsibilities of David and the twelve apostles will increase. Jesus Christ will be overseer and counselor. His word on any issue will be final.

Does God Love the Jew More Than the Gentile?

The New Testament reveals the wonderful truth of God's

The Millennium

universal love. He is "color-blind," meaning the Lord does not play favorites or love one race of people more than another. The Word says that in Him "there is neither Jew nor Greek, there is neither bond nor free, there is neither male nor female: for ye are all one in Christ Jesus" (Galatians 3:28).

The apostle Peter was a Jew who once considered Gentiles to be "common" and "unclean." He was a Jewish bigot until God dealt with his prejudice through a vision and subsequent visit to the home of a Gentile named Cornelius. In the vision, God commanded Peter to rise and eat certain things that were not kosher—things forbidden under Jewish law (Acts 10:11–13).

The point of the vision was not food per se; the Lord was telling Peter, "What God hath cleansed, that call not thou common" (Acts 10:15), speaking of the Gentiles. After pondering the vision, the apostle humbled himself and said "God hath shewed me that I should not call any man common or unclean" (Acts 10:28). Peter expressed this same sentiment in the home of Cornelius.

> Then Peter opened his mouth, and said, Of a truth I perceive that God is no respecter of persons: But in every nation he that feareth him, and worketh righteousness, is accepted with him. (Acts 10:34–35)

The reason for examining these verses in Acts is to make an important point. It would be easy for one to see how Israel will be blessed during the Millennium—Davidic kingdom restored, Christ ruling from Jerusalem, the twelve apostles ruling over the twelve tribes of Israel—and surmise God has more love for the Jew than the Gentile. This just isn't true. Although Israel is presently in a backslidden state, the Jews are covenant people. God made specific promises to these people, and unlike many of us, He keeps His promises.

> For by one Spirit are we all baptized into one body, whether we be Jews or Gentiles, whether we be bond or free; and have been all made to drink into one Spirit. (1 Corinthians 12:13)

The Twenty-Four Elders

Another group that will have great authority during the Millennium is the heavenly elders. When John was taken into heaven in Revelation 4, he stood upon what appeared to be "a sea of glass," looking out at God's throne. John saw that the mighty throne of God was surrounded by twenty-four smaller thrones. These thrones are for the twenty-four elders.

> And round about the throne were four and twenty seats: and upon the seats I saw four and twenty elders sitting, clothed in white raiment; and they had on their heads crowns of gold. (Revelation 4:4)

There is great mystery concerning these heavenly elders. We don't know who they are. We don't know why they deserve to be so close to God. We don't know if they are comprised of glorified Jews, glorified Gentiles, or a combination of the two. Setting these questions aside, one thing is certain: these heavenly elders hold powerful positions, and during the Millennium they will probably be second in command under Jesus Christ.

Works with Right Motives

The saints will indeed "possess the kingdom" during the Millennium. The government will be a theocracy (theonomy) under the divine power and authority of Jesus Christ: Jews

The Millennium

ruled by Christian Jewish leadership; Gentiles ruled by Christian Gentile leadership.

Unlike the restoration of the Davidic kingdom, Scripture doesn't reveal specific Gentile positions—who will rule over what. However, these positions will be filled according to the believer's faithfulness and spiritual works in this present age.

The Lord's criteria for millennial appointments will be solely based on the type of Christian life a believer now chooses to live. This doesn't settle well with those who put greater emphasis on grace than on works. But then the apathetic believer must understand that we are saved by grace *through faith unto good works*. In his epistle, James made it clear that faith without works is dead (James 2:20), that it is imperative for Christians to demonstrate their faith by works (James 2:18), for it is through works that faith is perfected, made alive and vibrant (James 2:22).

The importance of spiritual works in our daily lives, in their relationship to the coming millennial kingdom, was addressed by Christ. In Luke 19, Jesus tells the parable of a nobleman and his ten servants. The nobleman was leaving for a distant country in order to receive a kingdom. Prior to leaving, he entrusted money to his employees. Ten pounds were distributed to ten servants. Upon the nobleman's return, the servants were summoned and ordered to give an account of the money. The first servant had turned his one pound into ten pounds; and because of his faithfulness, he was given charge over ten cities in his master's new kingdom "because thou hast been faithful in a very little, have thou authority over ten cities," (Luke 19:17). The second servant had turned his pound into five pounds and was rewarded with five cities "and he said likewise to him, Be thou also over five cities," (Luke 19:19). Then there was the unfaithful, lukewarm, apathetic servant who did nothing with his lord's money. He received no reward, in fact, the pound he was responsible for was given to another, "And he said unto them that stood by, Take from him the pound, and give it to him that hath ten pounds," (Luke 19:24).

In this parable, the nobleman represents Jesus Christ; the ten servants are the church; and the money represents faith. Christ is in heaven, but one day He will return to establish His millennial kingdom. You and I (His servants) have been commanded to carry on with His work.

> Verily, verily, I say unto you, He that believeth on me, the works that I do shall he do also; and greater works than these shall he do; because I go unto my Father. (John 14:12)

God has given each believer a measure of faith (Romans 12:3), and it is up to each individual to determine what he is going to do with his faith. Just like the servants in the parable, Christians will have to give account, "every one of us shall give account of himself to God" (Romans 14:12).

> For we must all appear before the judgment seat of Christ; that every one may receive the things done in his body, according to that he hath done, whether it be good or bad. (2 Corinthians 5:10)

As servants of God, our attitude should not be works for gain: I'll do things for Jesus now in order to obtain a good seat in the Millennium! Self-serving motives do nothing but stain the heart, producing the very thing God hates to see in His people—pride and arrogance.

Works determine how Christians will serve in Christ's coming kingdom, but they will be works based on love and humility because the believer has made Jesus Christ the focal

The Millennium

point of his life. Because the Holy Spirit is alive in one's heart causing him to both will, and to do, Christ's good pleasure. Works with "right motives" is the whole key.

Financially giving is a work, but giving *to get* is not a right motive. There are Christians who have actually gone bankrupt because some religious shyster told them God would pour out a one hundred-fold financial blessing if they would sacrificially give a huge amount of money; referred to as a "vow of faith" or "seed faith." Giving with the motive of receiving is not good works. It perverts and distorts what true giving is meant to be.

Christian "works" and "giving" should always be based on pure, selfless motives. A believer gives food, clothing, shelter, money, time, and friendship not because of some pseudospiritual business investment, but because there are thousands of people hurting in this country, suffering in this world, who need to see the love and compassion of Christ flowing through God's people to meet their needs. What a powerful testimony that is! The reward for such giving is something money can't buy; it's the warm feeling and inner satisfaction of being used by God to bless others.

> Every man according as he purposeth in his heart, so let him give; not grudgingly, or of necessity: for God loveth a cheerful giver. (2 Corinthians 9:7)

There are more questions than biblical answers concerning the millennial Gentile governmental structure. We can be sure, however, that the faithfulness and servitude of Christians in this present age will determine what role they play, "I will give unto every one of you according to your works" (Revelation 2:23).

During the Millennium some Christians will be given great authority over nations and cities, but there will also be plenty of lower offices to fill, and Christ promised that those who partake in the first resurrection (the resurrection of the righteous) will reign with Him for a thousand years.

> Blessed and holy is he that hath part in the first resurrection: on such the second death hath no power, but they shall be priests of God and of Christ, and shall reign with him a thousand years. (Revelation 20:6)

Ruling with a Rod of Iron

The book of Revelation teaches us that Christ and those He puts in positions of authority will rule the world with a rod of iron.

> And he [the saint] shall rule them with a rod of iron; as the vessels of a potter shall they be broken to shivers: even as I received of my Father. (Revelation 2:27)

The latter part of this verse is an allusion to Psalm 2:9, "Thou shalt *break* them with a rod of iron; thou shalt dash them in pieces like a potter's vessel." *Breaking* the nations with a rod of iron is not to be confused with *ruling* with a rod of iron. The breaking down or smashing of nations (like pottery thrown on the floor) relates to Christ's Second Advent. These are the finishing touches of the "Day of the Lord," when Jesus forcefully punishes the nations and takes control of the entire world. "Ruling with a rod of iron" pertains to the full thousand-year reign of Christ on earth.

> And she [Israel] brought forth a man child [Christ], who was to rule all nations with a rod of iron: and her child was caught up unto God, and to his throne. (Revelation 12:5)

The Millennium

There's no doubt about it—the Millennium will be a theocracy, a divine dictatorship. But the fact that the world will be ruled with a rod of iron doesn't mean it will be ruled by oppressive, tyrannical totalitarianism. Ruling with a rod of iron is better understood as "shepherding with a scepter of godly absolutes." Christ is coming to bring peace, righteousness, and restoration to a deteriorating world full of sin and violence.

During the Millennium, there will be no dishonest politicians, judges, or lawyers. There will be no A.C.L.U., and no homosexual, radical feminist, or anti-Semitic movements. The rights of unborn children will be protected, the holocaust of the innocent ended. There will be no more spiritual deception, no false religions, no cults or the occult. The morally and ethically degenerate profiteers who today hide behind the word *censorship* will no longer be able to "peddle their poison." Philippians 4:8 will become the standard by which the media (radio, television, movies, and magazines) operate.

> Finally, brethren, whatsoever things are true, whatsoever things are honest, whatsoever things are just, whatsoever things are pure, whatsoever things are lovely, whatsoever things are of good report: if there be any virtue, and if there be any praise, think on these things. (Philippians 4:8)

The Millennium will be a time of peace and restoration, but Christ and His saints would not need to rule "with a rod of iron" if everyone were obedient and crimes were not committed. Coming out of the Great Tribulation will be millions of people who have not made Christ their personal Savior. These folks will be ruled with a rod of iron, meaning all sin and rebellion will be quickly, fairly, and forcefully dealt with. The guilty will not be able to hide behind lies or smooth-talking attorneys.

It's interesting to note, that although Satan's demonic influence will have been eradicated, sin will still be present in the world. This proves that the problem with mankind is not external but internal.

> For from within, out of the heart of men, proceed evil thoughts, adulteries, fornications, murders, thefts, covetousness, wickedness, deceit, lasciviousness, an evil eye, blasphemy, pride, foolishness: All these evil things come from within, and defile the man. (Mark 7:21–23)

"The devil made me do it" will not wash in the Millennium. Even today, all Satan can do is present us with temptations—the demonic "window dressings" of sin. It's up to each individual to choose whether they play, and that choice is made according to the condition of one's heart.

Life in the Millennium

The bedraggled people who survived the Great Tribulation will need a period of adjustment to acclimate to Christ's methods of restoration and government. They will also need time to get accustomed to living with glorified saints—a strange heavenly group who are human in form, but not in essence, ability, attitude, and wisdom.

The "heavenly being" will be different from the "human being" in several obvious ways: They cannot die or be killed. They will not suffer from the numerous emotional and physical maladies that afflict humans. The wisdom God imparted in the resurrection, rapture, and glorification—will far exceed anything that can be achieved through mere human endeavor. And the earthly physical laws that dictate human capability will not determine heavenly spiritual capability. Miraculous feats that transcend human ability will become everyday occurrences.

It may seem to some that with having all these superior, supernatural attributes, the heavenly saint may come across as an arrogant, egotistical demigod. Nothing could be further from the truth. Those kinds of negative characteristics reflect the nature of the one sitting in the bottomless pit, not the Lord of all creation! The glorified believer will exude God's love, patience, and righteousness. They will manifest the beautiful fruits of the Spirit in everything they do. Millennial citizens will perceive the "heavenly ones" as caring servants of Christ who are there to serve, not to be served.

During the Millennium, there will be glorified citizens, both Jewish and Gentile—and there will be human citizens, both Jewish and Gentile. Humanity will consist of born-again believers and those who have not given their hearts to the Lord. But whether one is Jewish or Gentile, human or heavenly, saved or unsaved—we will all delight in seeing a suffering world be transformed into the kind of world God originally intended. There will be rules and regulations to follow, but ones designed to work for the health, growth, and betterment of mankind, not against it. I, for one, am looking forward to life in the Millennium.

The Millennial Temple

Prior to the time when New Jerusalem descends upon a new earth, history will have seen five temples in Jerusalem: Solomon's temple, Zerubbabel's temple, Herod's temple, the tribulation temple, and the millennial temple.

Solomon's temple, Zerubbabel's temple, and Herod's temple were all in the past. The tribulation and millennial temples are in the future. We know there will be a temple standing during the Great Tribulation because of the *abomination of desolation*, when the Antichrist breaks his seven-year covenant with Israel, tramples the holy city Jerusalem, and desecrates the temple (Daniel 9:27; Matthew 24:15; 2 Thessalonians 2:4; Revelation 11:1–2). The final temple will be Christ's millennial temple. You can read all about this fascinating temple in Ezekiel 40–46.

> "Son of man, describe the temple [the Millennial Temple] to the people of Israel, that they may be ashamed of their sins. Let them consider the plan, and if they are ashamed of all they have done, make known to them the design of the temple—its arrangement, its exits and entrances—its whole design and all its regulations and laws. Write these down before them so that they may be faithful to its design and follow all its regulations." (Ezekiel 43:10–11 NIV)

Those in the church who deny a literal millennial temple (primarily amillennialists) use a twofold argument: First, they claim that the size of the temple is too large to sit atop Mount Moriah where the previous temples were located. Second, that the reinstatement of animal sacrifices violates New Testament Scripture (Hebrews 7:27; 9:11–15; 9:26; 10:10–12).

> We are sanctified through the offering of the body of Jesus Christ once for all. And every priest standeth daily ministering and offering oftentimes the same sacrifices, which can never take away sins: But this man, after he had offered one sacrifice for sins for ever, sat down on the right hand of God. (Hebrews 10:10–12)

The argument regarding the size of the millennial temple

The Millennium

loses credence when one considers the fact that Jerusalem's topography will be different following the Great Tribulation; the land complexion will not be the same. According to Revelation 16:19, following the greatest earthquake in history, the city of Jerusalem will be divided into three parts.

And in Zechariah 14:4 we discover at the Second Advent, when Christ stands on the Mount of Olives, it will split apart and travel in four different directions.

> And his feet shall stand in that day upon the mount of Olives, which is before Jerusalem on the east, and the mount of Olives shall cleave in the midst thereof toward the east and toward the west, and there shall be a very great valley; and half of the mountain shall remove toward the north, and half of it toward the south. (Zechariah 14:4)

Following the Great Tribulation there will be plenty of room for the millennial temple.

The argument that the reinstatement of animal sacrifices violates New Testament Scripture would be true if the purpose of the millennial sacrifices were to atone for sin. This is where the proponents of this argument miss the boat (so to speak).

Animal sacrifices never had, and never will have, the power to atone for sin. This means the millennial sacrifices will be no more expiatory (atoning) than the Old Testament sacrifices. Jesus Christ was the one true sacrificial Lamb—forever!

The Old Testament sacrifices had a *prospective* meaning; they were a *type* that pointed toward the cross as a foreshadowing of Christ's future sacrifice. The millennial sacrifices will have a *retrospective* meaning; they will be *commemorative*, pointing back at the cross as a constant reminder of the price of redemption. The ultimate sacrifice

Jesus Christ was willing to suffer for all of humanity. The Old Testament Sacrifices were *typical;* the millennial sacrifices will be *commemorative.*

In his book *The Revelation Record,* Dr. Henry M. Morris presents a sound millennial sacrifice explanation:

> Such animal sacrifices had been, of course, set aside after the death and resurrection of Christ, for "he had offered one sacrifice for sins for ever" (Hebrews 10:12). During the Christian dispensation, the gospel of salvation by grace through faith in Christ needed no animal sacrifices either as evidence of faith or as aid to faith. In the millennium, however, it will be different. It will be easy to believe in Christ—in fact almost impossible *not* to believe. No longer will one suffer ridicule or persecution if he takes a stand for Christ, nor will he ever be led astray by evolutionary teachings in the schools or by overt temptations to sin by his peers.
>
> In every dispensation, salvation is offered only by the grace of God on the basis of the substitutionary death of Christ for sin. Before His first coming people had given evidence of their faith in God's promised redemption by offering sacrificial animals in atonement for their sins. In that case, the sacrifices had served both as a significant aid to faith and as a testimony to their faith. Even in the Christian age "faith without works is dead" (James 2:20), but that faith is exercised in the person and finished work of Christ, as confirmed and recorded in the Holy Scriptures of the New Testament.
>
> In the millennial age, with the glorified Christ and His resurrected and reigning saints personally present and with Satan and his hosts out of the way, there will

be no room whatsoever for intellectual doubt as to the deity of Christ and the truth of His Word. Nevertheless, salvation will still require a *personal* faith and commitment to Christ and, more than ever, the genuineness of such faith must be evidenced by works. It may well be that this is at least part of the reason for the reinstitution of animal sacrifices. In the days of His humiliation, it requires strong faith to believe in His coming glorification. In the days of His glory, it will be difficult to remember and believe in His humiliation and death, and yet it is still as important as ever that men and women understand and believe that they are sinners and can only be saved through the substitutionary death of Christ for their sins. Thus, the animal sacrifices will be a memorial and reminder of the great saving work of Christ, and thus will also serve both as an aid and evidence of faith. [2]

The Temple Gates

The millennial temple will be the world's capitol building. It will have gates on the east, north, and south sides. After its construction, Jesus will enter through the east gate (Ezekiel 43:1–5) and take His presidential position on the throne of David.

> And, behold, thou shalt conceive in thy womb, and bring forth a son, and shalt call his name JESUS. He shall be great, and shall be called the Son of the Highest: and the Lord God shall give unto him the throne of his father David: And he shall reign over the house of Jacob for ever; and of his kingdom there shall be no end. (Luke 1:31–33)

The east gate will only be used by Christ and the temple priests. Public access will be through the north and south gates. There will also be a rather strange rule regarding the use of the temple gates: U-turns prohibited! If one enters through the north gate, he must exit through the south gate—and vice versa.

> When the people of the land come before the Lord at the appointed feasts, whoever enters by the north gate to worship is to go out the south gate; and whoever enters by the south gate is to go out the north gate. No one is to return through the gate by which he entered, but each is to go out the opposite gate. (Ezekiel 46:9 NIV)

The reason for this temple rule is probably to eliminate people from crossing twice over sacred ground (see the diagram on page 149).

Visits to the millennial temple will not be for sight-seeing tours, lunch meetings, or festive gatherings. When one enters the temple, he will be standing upon holy ground, in the presence and glory of the Lord. Humility, respect, and reverence will be the decorum. Temple visits will be a privilege with the sole purpose of worship and praise. How wonderful it will be to personally see our Lord and Savior, Jesus Christ, and receive His holy love, exhortation, admonition, and blessing. Requiring visitors to exit through the opposite gate they entered, even though transportation may be on the other side, is an inconvenience no one will complain about. (Who knows, there may even be a temple shuttle!)

The Millennium

The Feast of Tabernacles

The Feast of Tabernacles (also known as the Feast of Booths, the Feast of Ingatherings, the Feast of Tents, and the Feast of Jehovah) was an annual seven-day festival. Makeshift abodes called "booths" were made from branches and leaves to commemorate God's divine protection of the Hebrews during their exodus from Egypt and journey to Canaan.

During the Feast of Tabernacles the Jewish people lived in these rickety booths for seven full days, demonstrating that God would protect His people from both the elements and hostile environments. As they traveled through the desert, the Hebrews often faced adverse conditions, but God's presence was always there. The Feast of Tabernacles was also a celebration of the harvest—a joyous occasion for giving praise to the Lord and enjoying food.

During the Millennium, the Feast of Tabernacles will be celebrated every year. Since the Millennium is a thousand years, the church will partake in this festival a thousand times.

> And it shall come to pass, that every one that is left [after the War of Armageddon] of all the nations which came against Jerusalem shall even go up from year to year to worship the King, the Lord of hosts, and to keep the feast of tabernacles. (Zechariah 14:16)

It's interesting that a Jewish festival will become a universal celebration for both Jews and Gentiles. The Feast of Tabernacles will not be an option, but a commandment of Christ to all nations and peoples. There will be no excuse for not attending the feast! Any nation that refuses to make the annual pilgrimage to Jerusalem will be punished by having its rain cut off.

And it shall be, that whoso will not come up of all the families of the earth unto Jerusalem to worship the King, the Lord of hosts, even upon them shall be no rain....This shall be the punishment of Egypt, and the punishment of all nations that come not up to keep the feast of tabernacles. (Zechariah 14:17, 19)

Although a bit dated, this hip jargon seems to fit: "Be there, or be square!"

The Millennium
Temple Court

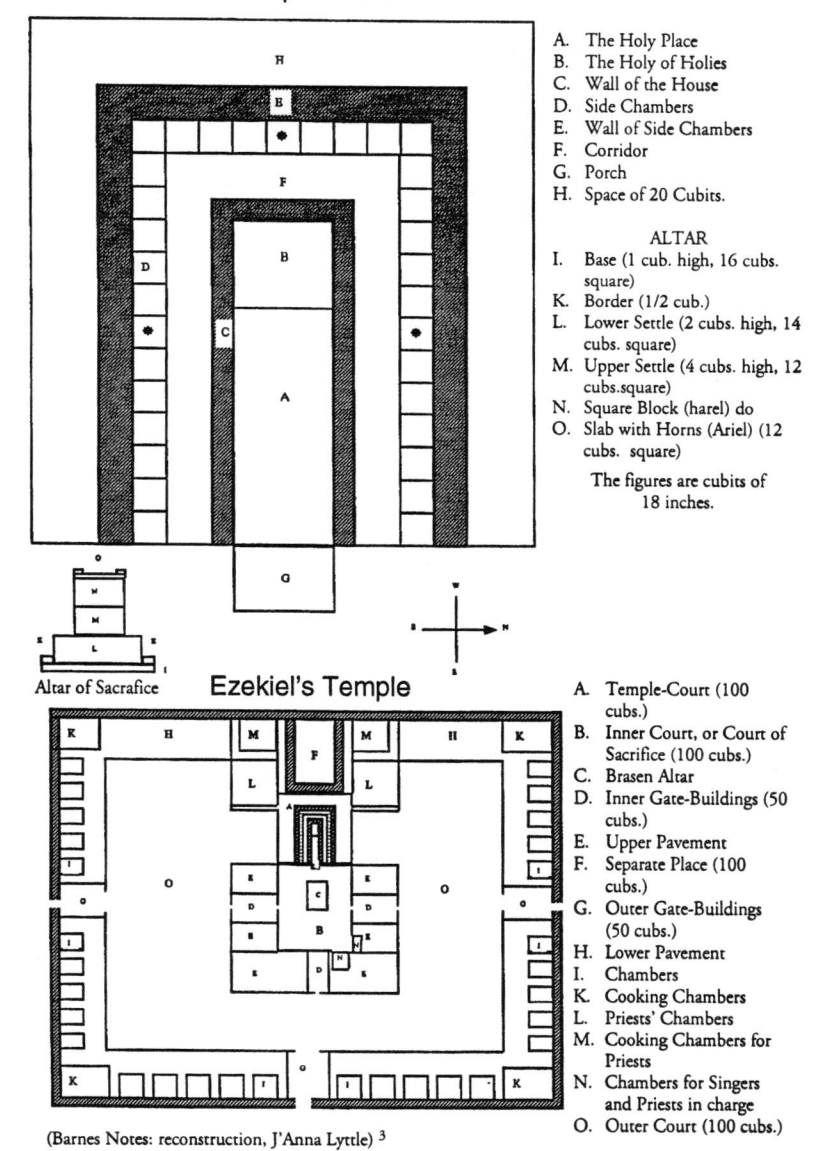

A. The Holy Place
B. The Holy of Holies
C. Wall of the House
D. Side Chambers
E. Wall of Side Chambers
F. Corridor
G. Porch
H. Space of 20 Cubits.

ALTAR
I. Base (1 cub. high, 16 cubs. square)
K. Border (1/2 cub.)
L. Lower Settle (2 cubs. high, 14 cubs. square)
M. Upper Settle (4 cubs. high, 12 cubs. square)
N. Square Block (harel) do
O. Slab with Horns (Ariel) (12 cubs. square)

The figures are cubits of 18 inches.

Altar of Sacrafice

Ezekiel's Temple

A. Temple-Court (100 cubs.)
B. Inner Court, or Court of Sacrifice (100 cubs.)
C. Brasen Altar
D. Inner Gate-Buildings (50 cubs.)
E. Upper Pavement
F. Separate Place (100 cubs.)
G. Outer Gate-Buildings (50 cubs.)
H. Lower Pavement
I. Chambers
K. Cooking Chambers
L. Priests' Chambers
M. Cooking Chambers for Priests
N. Chambers for Singers and Priests in charge
O. Outer Court (100 cubs.)

(Barnes Notes: reconstruction, J'Anna Lyttle) [3]

Chapter Eight

SATAN IS LOOSED "A LITTLE SEASON"

After the Millennium

Well, we just cruised through the time known as the Millennium. Christians will be resurrected, raptured, and glorified—then reign with Jesus Christ on this present earth for a period of one thousand years. You know, we humans are lucky to get seventy to eighty years out of this life. And if we add to those seventy to eighty years the time of the Millennium, where Christians will live more than ten human lifetimes, our life span becomes absolutely incredible!

Now let's take this one step further by comparing the

Satan Is Loosed "A Little Season"

thousand years with eternity, and the Millennium becomes little more than a drop in the bucket! I realize this can be a bit mind-boggling, a little hard to grasp—however, meditating upon an adventurous eternity with Jesus Christ certainly puts our present existence in its proper perspective.

In this chapter we will take a look at two significant events that occur at the end of the Millennium: Satan set free for "a little season," and the Great White Throne Judgment.

Satan Is Set Free

Two of the more difficult prophetic events to comprehend fully are the reinstatement of animal sacrifices during the Millennium and Satan being set free to deceive the nations at the end of this thousand-year period.

The millennial reign of Christ begins with an angel descending from heaven, "having the key of the bottomless pit and a great chain in his hand" (Revelation 20:1). The devil and his demonic kingdom of darkness will be bound in this "spirit prison" for a thousand years. At the end of the Millennium (prior to the Great White Throne Judgment and the creation of a new heaven, a new earth, and the descension of New Jerusalem) Satan is set free: "he must be loosed a little season" (Revelation 20:3). Scripture unequivocally states the reason for Satan's incarceration, "that he should deceive the nations no more" (Revelation 20:3).

The purpose of Christ's millennial reign is to bring peace, righteousness, and restoration to a world on the brink of annihilation. By the end of the thousand years, the earth will have been restored. Governments, businesses, judicial systems, and families will pretty much function the way God intended them to function. With Satan in the world, this could never be achieved. His power and influence are much too strong. If anyone should doubt this, consider the fact he gained the allegiance of one-third of God's holy angels—not on earth—but in heaven itself! To put it bluntly: Lucifer made more sense to these deceived angels than God.

Revelation 20:3 says that Satan "should deceive the nations no more, *till* the thousand years should be fulfilled." The devil will be set free in order to deceive the nations—to cause great disruption and chaos in a world to which Christ has brought peace and obedience. But why? Why would God allow the mighty restorative victory that Christ and the glorified saints obtained to be shattered? Why would He allow the evil deceptive power of "the father of lies" (John 8:44 NIV) to once again infiltrate the earth? Satan ripped off God in heaven, then ripped Him off on earth, and now he is given the opportunity to rip Him off at the end of the Millennium! But why?

Just like the reinstatement of animal sacrifices, this question is not answered in Scripture. Meaning there are no verses stating, "The animal sacrifices will be reinstated because of items one, two, and three," or, "Satan will be set free at the end of the Millennium because of items four, five, and six." To find a plausible answer to this perplexing question, one must first understand the purpose of the Millennium. As previously discussed, Christ's thousand-year reign will bring peace, righteousness, and restoration to a rebellious world that refused to live right. However, this will not be the "eternal earth"—the eternal kingdom of God. The Millennium is a transitory era between our present age and eternity, an eternity that only belongs to *true believers*. Herein lies the answer to our question—*true believers*.

The Millennium is a time of restoration. During this thousand-year period people will accept Jesus Christ as their

Satan Is Loosed "A Little Season"

Lord and Savior. But unlike Christians in this present age, there will not be much to test whether they have *true faith* or *said faith*. How much effort or devotion will it take to believe in Jesus when He is standing right there? How can true faith be determined if there is hardly any adversity or temptation? Christians throughout history have had their faith tested each and every day. We live in a sinful world full of trials and tribulations, with temptations around every corner. The adversary of our soul, the devil, "walketh about, seeking whom he may devour" (1 Peter 5:8), and his main target is the believer. He will do anything to make a Christian fall, attacking every wise decision that is made. He is not excited over the prospect of people inheriting the wonderful promises of God—things that were once his. Today, it takes a real man or woman of God to stand strong in faith. It takes a depth of love and commitment to the Savior—one that is clearly visible for all to see.

God's release of Satan from the bottomless pit will not be a "slap in the face" that is meant to negate all the positive things Christ accomplished during His thousand-year reign. It will simply be time to move on—time to judge the world and time for true believers to enter eternity.

Satan will test the loyalty and faith of millennial believers with trials, tribulations, lies, and temptations. This will result in a separation between those who only mouthed a few words, *said faith*, from those who possess true, enduring faith. Only the latter will be welcomed into God's beautiful eternal home. You've got to love it! Although Satan and his demonic kingdom work against God on every front, the Lord will actually use them for an extremely important purpose. Out of the devil's wickedness, the Lord brings forth good.

The Final War

It's sad that the legacy of man is a propensity toward greed, hate, bloodshed, and war. The old axiom is true: One thing men learn from history is that men don't learn from history! So, it should surprise no one that the future will see three major wars prophesied in Scripture:

1. The war described in Ezekiel 38–39. Gog and Magog (Russia) along with five other nations make war against Israel.

2. The War of Armageddon. This will be World War III in which many nations will be in conflict on the Plain of Megiddo, the Valley of Decision (also known as the Valley of Jehosphaphat).

3. The war described in Revelation 20. This war occurs at the end of the Millennium. The nations that fall prey to Satan's deceptive power attempt to make war against Jesus Christ and His glorified saints.

All three of these wars take place in Israel's neighborhood, but they all are distinctively different.

At the end of the thousand-year reign of Christ, Satan is loosed for a little season "to deceive the nations which are in the four quarters of the earth, Gog and Magog, to gather them together to battle" (Revelation 20:8). With Jesus Christ personally on earth, with loving saints ministering to millennial people, with a thriving world economy, with fair and honest Jewish and Gentile governments in place—the fact that Satan will be able to deceive nations into despising all these wonderful things is inexplicable! We are not talking about a small group of antisocials or a fringe gathering of unhappy campers. The number of millennial people who literally attempt to kill Jesus and His saints will be in the millions, "the number of whom is as the sand of the sea" (Revelation 20:8).

Satan Is Loosed "A Little Season"

What puts this event in complete irony, the actions of the people in obliquity, is after experiencing Christ's divine power, glory, and authority for one thousand years, they seem oblivious to the fact that Jesus and His saints cannot be killed. It's as though Satan slipped them a Mickey (drugged them) which rendered their mental faculties into "gray matter mush!" They somehow forgot that God and His heavenly host of angels, would never allow any sort of hostile invasion or governmental overthrow. The moment these misguided aggressors surround Jerusalem, they quickly learn this was not a good idea!

> And they went up on the breadth of the earth, and compassed the camp of the saints about, and the beloved city: and fire came down from God out of heaven, and devoured them. (Revelation 20:9)

Gog and Magog

Since Revelation 20 and Ezekiel 38–39 both mention Gog and Magog, some people conclude that the wars described in these passages are synonymous. Seeing Gog and Magog in Revelation 20 does pose a problem for interpretation; however, these battles are not identical.

The war in Ezekiel 38–39 describes Russia, along with five nations listed in Scripture—Persia (Iran), Ethiopia, Libya, Gomer (possibly Germany), and Togarmah (possibly Turkey)—attempting to invade Israel. In contrast, the war seen in Revelation 20 involves many nations of the world gathered against Jesus Christ and His saints. These two wars are separated by a period of approximately one thousand years.

Magog was the second son of Japheth and grandson of Noah (Genesis 10:1–2). He developed a great kingdom north of the Black and Caspian Seas. This area became known as Scythia, and today it is called Russia. Magog's brothers, Meshech and Tubal, also settled in parts of the north. "Meshech" may be modern-day Moscow; and "Tubal" could possibly be Tobolsk.

When Scripture speaks of Gog and Magog in regards to the war of Ezekiel 38—39 and the war of Revelation 20, it is speaking of a person, Gog, who is the leader of a people that reside in a land called Magog.

Since the Bolshevik Revolution in 1917, the Soviet Union has had several Gogs, beginning with Vladimir Ilich Lenin and Joseph Stalin. Believers will be able to identify the two "Gogs" of Ezekiel and Revelation when they come forward to fulfill their roles in Bible prophecy.

Israel will win the war of Ezekiel 38—39, but not because of military prowess. The invading military forces will be massive, well-armed, and capable of giving this tiny nation a sound thrashing!

> Thou shalt ascend and come like a storm, thou shalt be like a cloud to cover the land, thou, and all thy bands, and many people with thee. (Ezekiel 38:9)

Israel will emerge victorious, but not because of superior strategy or some other natural explanation. They will win because of God's supernatural intervention!

> And I [the Lord] will turn thee back, and leave but the sixth part of thee, and will cause thee to come up from the north parts, and will bring thee upon the mountains of Israel: And I [the Lord] will smite thy bow out of thy left hand, and will cause thine arrows to fall out of thy right hand. Thou shalt fall upon the mountains of Israel, thou, and all thy bands, and the people that is

with thee: I will give thee unto the ravenous birds of every sort, and to the beasts of the field to be devoured. (Ezekiel 39:2–4)

Following the Great Tribulation, Magog's population will be decimated. But by the end of the Millennium, they will probably have a greater population than before the war of Ezekiel 38—39. When Satan is released from the bottomless pit to deceive the nations, he will find the most willing ear in "Gog," and the most corrupt hearts in the people of "Magog." As in the war of Ezekiel 38—39, Gog and Magog will be leaders in the futile attack upon God's anointed.

How refreshing it will be to finally see the end of war and the end of bloodshed spawned by hatred, greed, selfishness, and prejudice. Revelation 20:8–9 will be mankind's final battle—although "battle" or "war" may not be appropriate terms. Christ and His saints will not lift a finger against this ill-advised invasion. The only casualties will be to those who foolishly surround Jerusalem, "And fire came down from God out of heaven, and devoured them." These deceived people will learn what those who perished in the Great Tribulation learned. The price of rebellion—the cost of having an unrepentant heart—is indeed very steep!

Satan Cast into the Lake of Fire

Following the final war, Satan will be cast into the lake of fire.

> And the devil that deceived them was cast into the lake of fire and brimstone, where the beast and the false prophet are, and shall be tormented day and night for ever and ever. (Revelation 20:10)

There is something noteworthy in Revelation 20:10 that you and I can use to refute those (such as the Jehovah's Witnesses) who deny the biblical concept of an eternal hell. The Jehovah's Witnesses teach the false doctrine of *annihilation*, which says that those who are sent to the lake of fire are annihilated—meaning they no longer exist in any way, shape, or form.

If you'll remember, the Antichrist (the beast) and the False Prophet were cast into the lake of fire directly after the War of Armageddon. Yet here in Revelation 20:10 we see them still alive after spending one thousand years in eternal hell, "And the devil that deceived them was cast into the lake of fire and brimstone, where the beast and the false prophet *are*."

The casting of Satan into eternal hell is his final judgment. There will be no pardons or reprieves. The sentence is eternal, the lake of fire internment will last forever. Never again will the devil or his demons see the beauty of God's creation. Never again will they tempt, influence, possess, or harass another soul. A fitting end to evil spirits so vile and wicked.

The Great White Throne Judgment

Following the millennial age, God will literally incinerate both heaven (meaning our universe) and earth.

> But the day of the Lord will come as thief in the night; in the which the heavens shall pass away with a great noise, and the elements shall melt with fervent heat, the earth also and the works that are therein shall be burned up. (2 Peter 3:10)

The annihilation of the universe creates a void in which God places His *Great White Throne*.

And I saw a great white throne, and him that sat on it,

Satan Is Loosed "A Little Season"

from whose face the earth and the heaven fled away; and there was found no place for them. (Revelation 20:11)

A theory I have long subscribed to is that the third heaven (God's home) is not parked out beyond Pluto somewhere, but instead exists in a different dimensional world. If true, this would explain why heaven and New Jerusalem are not affected by the fiery explosion that obliterates the universe.

My good friend, Robert Faid, who is both a Christian author and nuclear scientist, examines the intriguing possibility of heaven existing in a different dimensional world in his book, *A Scientific Approach to Biblical Mysteries.*

> In our world every bit of matter and energy is governed by the four fundamental forces which operate in the three physical dimensions in which we are enclosed. These three dimensions are our boundaries, and we cannot escape from them. Everything from a single atom within our own bodies to an exploding supernova a billion light years from the earth is confined within these limiting dimensions.
>
> This is *our* world, but in John 18:36, Jesus answered Pilate's question by saying, "My kingdom is not of this world."
>
> God is certainly *not* confined to only our dimensional limitations. In 2 Chronicles 2:6 we read Solomon's reflection on the magnitude of God, "But who is able to build him a house, seeing the heaven and heaven of heavens cannot contain Him?"
>
> We find right in His Word, a reference to the fact that God's kingdom—heaven—is *not* of this world, and that even the heavens of heavens cannot contain Him, for He transcends all physical limitations.

From this we can conclude that since God's abode of heaven is not located within the three dimensional limits of our world, then it must be located *outside* of it.

Our universe is structured on three physical dimensions, plus the additional dimension of time. There is no way that our particular dimensions may be *extended* outside of our universe, but suppose the dimension of time is transcendent—not limited to our own universe—and shared mutually by worlds outside of our own. If, as calculations indicate, there is a total of ten possible dimensions, if we subtract the three that define our universe, plus time, that leaves six dimensions left over.

Three of the the remaining dimensions *could* be the location of heaven.

Since each of these "heavenly" dimensions would be at right angles to those of our own, *heaven could occupy exactly the same space as our own world does.*

In other words, it is mathematically possible that the earth and heaven exist simultaneously in the same space, but with dimensions at right angles to each other. It is impossible for us to visualize this mentally, for we are conditioned to think only in the dimensions of our own universe, but this is mathematically possible.[1]

I recommend reading chapter 20 of Bob's fascinating book so you can get the entire gist of this amazing concept.

At the Great White Throne Judgment our whole three-dimensional universe will be in transition. Nothing will inhabit space except God, His white throne, and those being judged. Following the judgment the Lord will usher in an eternity of righteousness for all His people. He will fill this void with a new universe, a new earth, and upon this new earth He will place the heavenly city, New Jerusalem.

There is a difference of opinion as to who actually performs the judging: God the Father, or God the Son—First or Second Person of the Trinity? Those who believe Jesus Christ will judge use John 5:22 as proof text, "For the Father judgeth no man, but hath committed all judgment unto the Son." I don't know if the context of John chapter 5 supports the idea of Jesus as the white throne judge. It is an interesting but moot issue. While the identity of the judge is debatable, the ones being judged are clearly recognizable. The Great White Throne Judgment is the judgment of damnation.

Two Resurrections and Two Deaths

The first resurrection is the resurrection of the righteous who will stand before the judgment seat (Bema Seat) of Christ. The second resurrection is the resurrection of the wicked who will stand before God at the Great White Throne Judgment. A thousand years separate these two resurrections, "Blessed and holy is he that hath part in the first resurrection: on such the second death hath no power" (Revelation 20:6). Only those who are part of the second resurrection—the ones judged at the white throne—will experience the "second death."

First Death

Everyone must physically die once. Even those who are raptured alive must shed their "earth suits." When Christians die, their souls and spirits go into the paradise of God, "to be absent from the body [is] to be present with the Lord" (2 Corinthians 5:8).

When the unrighteous die, their souls and spirits go into Hades to wait for the Great White Throne Judgment.

Second Death
The second resurrection occurs following the thousand-year millennial period. God will release the souls and spirits from Hades, insert them into their restored (or recreated) bodies, then bring them before His Great White Throne.

Subsequent to the judgment, the unsaved will be cast into the lake of fire where their bodies will die a second time, *a second death*, but their souls and spirits will live on forever.

In Revelation 19:20, we see that the Antichrist and the False Prophet "both were cast *alive* into a lake of fire burning with brimstone." Their physical bodies certainly died in hell, but their souls and spirits will never die.

Why the Judgment?

If everyone judged at the Great White Throne Judgment is cast into Gehenna, why will there be a judgment? When judgment comes, why doesn't God just toss these people into eternal hell and be done with it? Because the judgment of both the righteous and unrighteous is based upon works, and these works determine the eternal position of the individual, "and they were judged every man according to their works" (Revelation 20:13).

First Corinthians 3 teaches that the eternal position and reward of the believer is determined solely by works. If a Christian's foundation is Christ, but his spiritual works are "wood, hay, and stubble" (wrong theology, wrong motives, and spiritual apathy), that person should not expect to receive much in God's kingdom.

If, on the other hand, a believer's foundation is Christ, and his or her spiritual works are "gold, silver, and precious stones" (spiritual vibrancy, sound doctrine, and godly motives), he or she will receive a much higher position.

Satan Is Loosed "A Little Season"

Every man's work shall be made manifest: for the day shall declare it, because it shall be revealed by fire; and the fire shall try every man's work of what sort it is. (1 Corinthians 3:13)

The judgment of hell will also be based on works. Do you think it would be fair if Aunt Sue, who lived a relatively decent life but rejected Christ's atonement, received the exact punishment and judgment of serial killers and child molesters? Of course not! That is why God will not just blindly throw everyone into eternal hell. That's why there will be a Great White Throne Judgment.

Scripture doesn't explicitly describe different locations or levels of punishment in hell, but it is clearly indicated and logically consistent. It certainly reflects the fairness of God and provides an explanation for a White Throne Judgment.

The Judgment

"Every knee shall bow, every tongue confess, that Jesus Christ is Lord," are words joyfully sung and positively expressed in songs, poems, and sermons. These words are cheerfully uttered without the slightest thought that they relate to the darkest day in human history—the "day of reckoning," the Great White Throne Judgment. Verses such as: Isaiah 45:23; Romans 14:11; and Philippians 2:10–11 will not be fulfilled until the judgment of damnation.

> For it is written, As I live, saith the Lord, every knee shall bow to me, and every tongue shall confess to God. (Romans 14:11)

Though it will be too late for salvation, everyone who refused to acknowledge God or accept Jesus as Savior will bow before God and Christ at the Great White Throne. The ungodly rantings of atheists will be silenced. The rhetoric of evolutionists will not be heard. The praise and exaltation of Buddha, Allah, Krishna, or any heathen god, demigod, false christ, or false prophet will not enter the throne room.

Every knee shall bow, every tongue shall confess that God is Creator and Jesus Christ is Savior. Excuses for rejecting the love and grace of God will not be accepted. If someone were to plead, "But Lord, I just didn't know!" they would probably hear, "Oh, but you should have known!"

> For since the creation of the world God's invisible qualities—his eternal power and divine nature—have been clearly seen, being understood from what has been made, so that men are without excuse. (Romans 1:20 NIV)

No matter why, when, where, or how unsaved people die, they will all be resurrected and stand before the Great White Throne. God will open the Book of Life, which contains the names of all saved people, and He will open other books that pertain to those being judged.

> And I saw the dead, small and great, stand before God; and the books were opened: and another book was opened, which is the book of life: and the dead were judged out of those things which were written in the books, according to their works. (Revelation 20:12)

It is amazing to think that God has recorded each and every moment of our lives, whether we are saved or not. He knows us better than we know ourselves, for "nothing in all creation is hidden from God's sight. Everything is uncovered and laid bare before the eyes of him to whom we must give account" (Hebrews 4:13 NIV).

Satan Is Loosed "A Little Season"

The entire lives of those at the Great White Throne Judgment will be laid out before them. They will see all the spiritual opportunities God graciously offered: to have faith; to become born-again; to have a personal relationship with the Lord; to be a partaker of Christ's inheritance; and to receive the free gift of everlasting life in heaven. But sadly, they will also see how "sin and rebellion" caused them to turn their backs on God and how it caused them to reject the sacrifice Christ made for them on the Cross. God will show the unredeemed that instead of listening to the truth about life and death, they chose to harden their hearts, close their ears, and say to the Lord, by either word or action—no thanks!

People will enter Gehenna—the lake of fire—eternal hell—fully comprehending why. There will be no arguments...just tears.

Do We Care?

There is not one person reading this book who doesn't have friends or relatives who will stand before God at the Great White Throne Judgment unless a change of heart is made. It hurts, doesn't it? None of us wants our loved ones to be eternally separated from God—to miss out on the splendor and joy of the new heaven, new earth, and the eternal city, "New Jerusalem."

I believe one of the reasons the Lord graphically reveals the destiny of unbelievers is to create in us, His people, hearts that truly care about lost souls. Many Christians fail to witness their faith because they are afraid of an adverse response. They don't want to stir the waters, rock the boat, or strain relationships. However, the last thing I ever want to experience is the eyes of a friend piercing through me at the Great White Throne

Judgment, and hear him say, "Terry, you knew all about salvation, heaven and hell, but you didn't love me enough to say anything."

Please join me in making a new commitment to reaching lost souls. To say, "Yes Lord, I do care enough to tell people the truth about life and death." In light of eternity, it really doesn't matter how people respond or how we are perceived. What matters is that on the Day of Judgment, our precious friends and family members will not be able to accuse us of having selfish hearts that refused to speak the truth.

Chapter Nine

NEW HEAVEN AND EARTH

In addition to talking about the new heaven and earth, this chapter will present two panoramic views of biblical history and prophecy: the long road of time and change, and the apostle John's experience on the island of Patmos where he received the book of Revelation. This is a bit parenthetical, but it all relates to the fabulous future God has revealed in His Word.

Long Road of Time and Change

From the book of Genesis through the book of Revelation, the Bible can panoramically be seen as a long road of time and change. Time and change has been both a friend and nemesis to man: a friend when God's divine will is obeyed; a nemesis when sin and rebellion stir the Lord to wrath and judgment.

Adam and Eve began traveling this road in the Garden of Eden, but when they fell, this freshly paved highway became a rocky road. A curse was placed upon the earth resulting in a loss of immortality. Eternal life on a perfect earth would not occur again until man's long, arduous journey on the road of time and change had been completed.

When Noah entered this road, he was forced to take a detour. No, the bridge wasn't out; the whole world was out! Because humanity had become so vile and wicked, God chose to make a new beginning. Noah, his family, and the animals all entered the ark and were placed back upon the long road of time and change following the flood.

As the road coursed through the Old Testament and the major and minor prophets, the Hebrews experienced many adversities. However, they were covenant people who found enduring faith through God's promise of a Messiah who would bring to the world an everlasting kingdom of righteousness.

Following the last word of the prophet Malachi, the road to eternity—the long road of time and change—came to a bridge. This bridge is approximately four hundred years long. These years are known as the "silent years," and they span the time between the Old and New Testaments. The road would not begin again until a young Jewish woman named Mary had been supernaturally impregnated by the Holy Spirit. She was told to name the child "Jesus," that He would be the Messiah called "Emmanuel, *God is with us.*"

The road which began in the Garden of Eden had now become a New Testament road. It was still rocky, but Jesus Christ filled in a few potholes with His transitional teachings from an old to a new dispensation, from the condemnation of the law to justification by grace.

Through the atonement, Jesus Christ became the "toll gate" through which the road to eternity traveled, "I am the way, the truth, and the life: no man cometh unto the Father, but by me" (John 14:6). The Messiah, Jesus Christ, reaffirmed the Old Testament promise of an everlasting kingdom for all of God's people.

> Then shall the King say unto them on his right hand, Come, ye blessed of my Father, inherit the kingdom prepared for you from the foundation of the world. (Matthew 25:34)

Moving through the New Testament: the synoptic Gospels, Gospel of John, Acts of the Apostles, Pauline, and other New Testament epistles, another road emerges traveling in the opposite direction. It is wide and quite attractive. The traffic is heavy, but the people seem oblivious as to where it is actually going.

This alluring highway is paved with a host of secular and religious philosophies that are antithetical to God's Word and will. The father of lies—the deceiver of souls—Satan himself, stands at the on ramp of this "highway to hell," offering the same variety of fruit with which Eve was deceived: "You shall not surely die, for the day you enter my road your perspectives will broaden; your horizons will widen; your experiences will be increased; and all your desires will be fulfilled. Hey, you don't need God, because *ye shall be as gods!*"

God's road is not as appealing to the flesh because it is a narrow road—a road narrowed by firm standards, narrowed by moral, ethical, and spiritual accountability. This is why those who travel the narrow way, the way that goes through the "toll gate" of Christ, are admonished to *walk in the Spirit,* not in the flesh; to *live in the Spirit,* not in the carnal ways of this world; and to be *led by the Spirit,* not by the dictates of the lower nature.

While the world makes things confusing, God makes it incredibly simple: two roads, two choices, two eternal destinies.

> Enter ye in at the strait gate: for wide is the gate, and broad is the way, that leadeth to destruction, and many there be which go in thereat: Because strait is the gate, and narrow is the way, which leadeth unto life, and few there be that find it. (Matthew 7:13–14)

Following the Great Tribulation and the War of Armageddon, the road to eternity drastically improves as it slowly meanders through the millennial reign of Christ. "Peace," "prosperity," and "restoration" will be the operative words during this thousand-year period. However, even though Satan's kingdom of darkness and his deceptive "highway to hell," has been imprisoned in the bottomless pit (not to surface again until the end of the Millennium) and even though saints are clothed in glorified bodies and living beautiful lives with Jesus Christ, the hearts of believers will long for the day when God creates an everlasting home for Him and all His children. This eternal home will be on a new earth, in a new universe, in a magnificent city called New Jerusalem.

> And I heard a great voice out of heaven saying, Behold, the tabernacle of God is with men, and he will dwell with them, and they shall be his people, and God himself shall be with them, and be their God. (Revelation 21:3)

As the long road of time and change nears the end of the

New Heaven and Earth

Millennium, excitement stirs the soul as the signposts read: "ETERNITY, 100 years; ETERNITY, 50 years—20 years, 10 years..." then all of a sudden the road that began in the Garden of Eden mysteriously disappears as God catapults His people through the threshold of eternity, through the portals of glory, gently placing them inside New Jerusalem which sits upon a new earth.

Eternity cannot be described as a new age, era, dispensation, or phase. Time and change as we know it now will simply not exist.

New Heaven and Earth

And I saw a new heaven and a new earth: for the first heaven and the first earth were passed away; and there was no more sea. (Revelation 21:1)

When this present universe is annihilated, there will be nothing but a vast void. God will temporarily place His Great White Throne in this nothingness. Then, following the judgment of damnation, a whole new universe and a brand new earth will emerge.

Sitting outside on a warm summer night, one cannot help but admire the beauty of God's creation—the moon, planets, and stars. The universe itself proves the existence of God, "The heavens declare the glory of God; and the firmament sheweth his handywork" (Psalm 19:1). The beauty of God's creation is here for man to enjoy, contemplate, and explore. I imagine God is well pleased when new discoveries are made within what He has created.

Scripture is silent as to what the new universe will be composed of. Will it have planets, moons, stars, or galaxies? Or will it be far removed from anything our present finite minds can comprehend or relate to? There are certainly more questions than answers, but we can be confident that the new universe will be breathtakingly beautiful.

Some believe there will not be a newly created earth. Instead they believe that our present earth will be restored or renovated. I do not accept this idea because Scripture strongly supports a newly created earth. The time of restoration occurs during the millennial reign of Jesus Christ. At the end of the thousand years, this earth will have served its purpose. Christ Himself said, "Heaven and earth shall pass away, but my words shall not pass away" (Matthew 24:35). Revelation 20:11 states, "The earth and the heaven fled away," and 2 Peter tells us the method by which God will destroy the heavens and the earth.

> But the day of the Lord will come as a thief in the night; in the which the heavens shall pass away with a great noise, and the elements shall melt with fervent heat, the earth also and the works that are therein shall be burned up. Seeing then that all these things shall be dissolved, what manner of persons ought ye to be in all holy conversation and godliness, Looking for and hasting unto the coming of the day of God, wherein the heavens being on fire shall be dissolved, and the elements shall melt with fervent heat? Nevertheless we, according to his promise, look for new heavens and a new earth, wherein dwelleth righteousness. (2 Peter 3:10–13)

Notice in Revelation 21:1 the new earth is described as having "no more sea." Our present earth is mostly covered with water. This signifies that the new eternal earth will not be our present earth.

New Heaven and Earth

Will We Remember Our Previous Lives?

Scripture does not supply much information regarding the new universe and earth, but Isaiah 65:17 does reveal a most interesting fact.

> For, behold, I create new heavens and a new earth: and the former shall not be remembered, nor come into mind. (Isaiah 65:17)

When God transports His people from the Millennium into eternity (i.e., to the new earth), much of our memory will be erased. The reason for this is obvious. The new heavens and earth will be created as a reward for the faithful and a new beginning for God and His people, a beginning that has no end. All the ugly stains of humanity, the negative things we saw, heard, and experienced on the old earth, will be removed from our minds. The hatred and violence, the crime, wars, murder, sin, and rebellion "shall not be remembered, nor come into mind."

How truly wonderful this will be! Have you noticed that when a past negative experience crosses our mind, we relive the incident a bit, often feeling the same pain? This will never happen in eternity. All negativity associated with our past life on the old earth can never again hurt, haunt, tempt, or hold any kind of mental or emotional grip. It will be as though our lives have always been full of perpetual joy.

Having our memory erased does not mean we will become new individuals with new minds. Not at all. Christians will be the same glorified people they were during the Millennium. God just clears out the mud and crud, so true continual happiness can become a reality. What a wonderful God we serve!

HAND GUIDE TO THE FUTURE

What An Experience!

The greatest experience of any Biblical figure has to be that of the apostle John on the island of Patmos. Patmos is situated between Turkey and Greece in the Aegean Sea. It belongs to a group of islands called *Sporades*. The island itself is relatively small, approximately seven miles long by four miles wide. Patmos was like an ancient Alcatraz or McNeil Island. It was a prison for criminals and those pesky creatures called Christians! In A.D. 95, the Roman emperor Domitian sentenced the apostle to this rocky island of hard labor. Patmos was riddled with mines in which the prisoners were forced to work.

But what was John's crime? Was he a rapist or thief? A murderer or child molester? Was he the godfather, the ringleader of some crime syndicate making "offers people could not refuse?" No, the remaining apostle from the original twelve (the others suffered martyrdom) was banished to Patmos because he had the audacity to witness Jesus Christ and preach the gospel.

> I John, who also am your brother, and companion in tribulation, and in the kingdom and patience of Jesus Christ, was in the isle that is called Patmos, for the word of God, and for the testimony of Jesus Christ. (Revelation 1:9)

John was in prayer on the Lord's Day—a day set aside for worship. I imagine he had a special place where he could pray and appreciate the magnificent beauty of the Aegean Sea and shoreline of Patmos. It is in prayer where John's fantastic journey began.

While he was praying, the apostle heard a voice as loud as a trumpet. To John it sounded like a gushing waterfall—"the

New Heaven and Earth

sound of many waters" (Revelation 1:15). The voice belonged to Jesus Christ. And when the apostle's eyes beheld the divine glory of the Lord, he "fell at his feet as dead." Jesus tells him to "fear not" (Revelation 1:17), then explains the reason for the visitation.

> Write the things which thou hast seen, and the things which are, and the things which shall be hereafter. (Revelation 1:19)

The apostle began receiving the book of Revelation on earth where Jesus dictated seven letters to the seven churches in Asia: Ephesus, Smyrna, Pergamos, Thyatira, Sardis, Philadelphia, and Laodicea. These letters found in Revelation 2 and 3 represent "the things which are." The remainder of the book (Revelation 4—22) is all prophetic, dealing specifically with events related to the end of this present age, the Millennium, and eternity.

After the seven letters to the seven churches in Asia were received, Jesus disappeared and a door opened up to heaven. As the apostle looked up through this heavenly doorway, a voice summoned, "Come up hither, and I will shew thee things which must be hereafter" (Revelation 4:1). John then probably had what is known as an out-of-body experience.

> And immediately I was in the spirit: and, behold, a throne was set in heaven, and one sat on the throne. (Revelation 4:2)

Interjection of Warning

John's possible out-of-body experience is not to be confused with the demonic practice of *astral projection,* nor is it something Christians should attempt to do. It's important to understand that this apostle didn't make a conscious effort to leave his body. He didn't light candles in a dark room, speak forth incantations, go into a self-induced trance, or perform some sort of spiritual ceremony.

No matter how many biblical words are used, if Christians dabble in soul travel, they have entered into the realm of the occult. Any experience achieved would be demonic. Having mastered several soul travel techniques prior to my conversion, I know of which I speak. It is of the devil! It is spiritual perversion!

I mention this because I have heard many testimonies given by people in Christian ministry who glorify such experiences. They publicly testify of their supposed celestial journeys, such as "trips to heaven," without giving any qualifications whatsoever. This is extremely dangerous! Good Christians are often duped into believing these individuals are "spiritual giants"—their teachings must be accurate—for after all, they had an experience similar to Paul and John. Beware of those in the church who are constantly having mystical experiences and one-to-one conversations with God, "I say to God, then He says to me" kind of nonsense.

Back to John's Experience

The apostle's spiritual adventure continues on in heaven where John stands before a sea of glass looking out at God and His throne, the twenty-four heavenly elders and their thrones, and the four living creatures who are probably cherubs. These living creatures will introduce the four horsemen of the apocalypse.

In Revelation 5, God holds up the book of seven seals, and

New Heaven and Earth

an angel issues a bold challenge: "Who is worthy to open the book, and loose the seals thereof?" Of course, Jesus Christ is the only one worthy enough to take the book and release the seals, "the Lion of the tribe of Juda, the Root of David, hath prevailed to open the book, and to loose the seven seals thereof" (Revelation 5:5). It's as though John were sitting in a movie theater with Technicolor and surround stereo sound as Jesus releases the first four seals and the living creatures command the four horsemen to come forward and reveal their purpose.

In Revelation 6, under the fifth seal, John saw martyred saints pleading with the Lord to avenge their blood, "How long, O Lord, holy and true, dost thou not judge and avenge our blood on them that dwell on earth?" (Revelation 6:10). They did not have to wait long, for God's wrath begins with the opening of the sixth seal.

> For the great day of his wrath is come; and who shall be able to stand? (Revelation 6:17)

In A.D. 95, John could not possible identify with all the technological advancement the world has made in two thousand years. Many of the things he witnessed had to be very confusing. However—war, persecution, judgment, and death are things anyone could comprehend no matter if they occurred in 1500 B.C. or in A.D. 2000. I'm sure it wasn't pleasant for John to witness the Great Tribulation period—the pouring out of God's wrath through the sixth seal, the seven trumpets, and the seven vials.

During this grievous time of observing the Great Tribulation, God graciously infused some parenthetical events which I'm sure the apostle appreciated. He was privileged to see the 144,000 Christian Jews selected and anointed for ministry. Twelve thousand from each of the twelve tribes of Israel were chosen and given God's seal of protection, "And I heard the number of them which were sealed: and there were sealed an hundred and forty and four thousand of all the tribes of the children of Israel" (Revelation 7:4). John was also privileged to see the powerful ministry of Christ's two witnesses.

> And I will give power unto my two witnesses, and they shall prophesy a thousand two hundred and threescore days, clothed in sackcloth. (Revelation 11:3)

John began receiving the last book of the Bible on earth, on the island of Patmos. He was then taken in the Spirit to heaven where he received (witnessed) Revelation 4—16. In Revelation 17, he is transported to a new location (possibly back to earth), to observe the destruction of end-time Babylon—which actually occurs in chapter 18.

> And there came one of the seven angels which had the seven vials, and talked with me, saying unto me, Come hither; I will shew unto thee the judgment of the great whore that sitteth upon many waters...So he carried me away in the spirit into the wilderness...(Revelation 17:1, 3a)

The apostle John witnessed the wrap-up of this present age: the War of Armageddon, the Second Advent of Christ, the casting of Satan's two advocates (the Antichrist and the False Prophet) into Gehenna, and the binding of the devil in the bottomless pit. He watched as Jesus Christ established a thousand-year reign of peace, and he saw how at the end of the Millennium the devil disrupts this peace when he is "loosed a little season." John observed how the nations of the world will be deceived into one final war, which could be appropriately called *the war of futility*, and how Satan finally receives his just deserts.

New Heaven and Earth

> And the devil that deceived them was cast into the lake of fire and brimstone, where the beast and the false prophet are, and shall be tormented day and night for ever and ever. (Revelation 20:10)

I would like to make a quick interjection here. Those who spend time in the book of Revelation, the Gospel of John, and John's three epistles (1, 2, and 3 John) cannot help but develop respect and admiration for this apostle. His love, obedience, and commitment to God, his demonstration of the fruits of the Spirit are things of spiritual beauty. It will be an honor to be able to meet him in heaven and personally express our sincere gratitude.

Can you imagine the expression on John's face as he witnessed the entire universe disappear? His bewilderment would then give way to solemnness as God manifests His Great White Throne, and the judgment of damnation begins. Following judgment, John saw a new heaven and earth emerge.

> And I saw a new heaven and a new earth: for the first heaven and the first earth were passed away; and there was no more sea" (Revelation 21:1)

What an experience!

Chapter Ten

NEW JERUSALEM

Have you ever thought about heaven in terms of what and where it actually is? Presently, we know that the paradise of God is heaven, or at least a big part of it. But there is coming a day when heaven will be upon a new earth, in a new universe. And upon this new earth will be a heavenly city called "New Jerusalem."

New Jerusalem: Heavenly Bride or Eternal City?

In Revelation 21, John saw New Jerusalem descending upon a new earth.

And I John saw the holy city, new Jerusalem, coming

New Jerusalem

down from God out of heaven, prepared as a bride adorned for her husband. (Revelation 21:2)

Since this verse states New Jerusalem comes down from heaven "as a bride adorned for her husband," and Revelation 21:9 says, "I will shew thee the bride, the Lamb's wife" (which also refers to the holy city), some expositors conclude New Jerusalem is not a literal city, but instead an allegory describing God's people—the *bride of Christ*. However, I believe New Jerusalem is a duality representing both the *bride of Christ* and the *eternal city*.

Those who deny a literal city have extreme difficulty interpreting, or better said, *spiritualizing*, the precise details Scripture reveals about New Jerusalem—its size, composition, and contents. The question allegorists cannot logically answer is: Why would Scripture describe the size of the city, its twelve foundations, the gates and wall, what construction material was used—further proclaiming that the throne of God and Christ are inside the city—if New Jerusalem is not a literal city, but instead just an allegory describing God's people? A guy would go nuts trying to spiritualize every facet of New Jerusalem. My allegorization would certainly be different from yours.

The bride aspect of New Jerusalem comes from Revelation 19 where we see the fabulous wedding feast and the marriage of the Lamb. This is a joyous celebration when the husbandman (Jesus Christ) marries His bride, the church.

> Let us be glad and rejoice, and give honour to him; for the marriage of the Lamb is come, and his wife hath made herself ready. (Revelation 19:7)

The Lord puts such significance to the relationship between the bride (His people) and New Jerusalem (His city) that in Revelation 3, He tells us the name "New Jerusalem" will be written upon the hearts of those who inherit the new earth.

Him that overcometh will I make a pillar in the temple of my God, and he shall go no more out: And I will write upon him the name of my God, *and the name of the city of my God, which is new Jerusalem,* which cometh down out of heaven from my God: and I will write upon him my new name. (Revelation 3:12)

When Scripture talks about the eternal city, New Jerusalem, it can be seen from two perspectives. When we mention a city—be it New York, Los Angeles, or any city—we're not just referring to buildings, asphalt, and cement. People are what make a city a city. New Jerusalem will personify the holiness and beauty of those who dwell there. When John saw New Jerusalem descending upon the new earth, he saw it as beautiful wedding garments that covered the bride inside. There is an old commercial that said, "With Certs, you get two mints in one!" Well, with New Jerusalem, you get a "city and people as one!"

God Shall Live with His People

We humans are finite, created beings. As such, it is impossible to fully comprehend the omnipresence of an eternal God or this divine attribute in relation to His home in heaven, to wit: If God is everywhere at all times, how can He live in heaven—a particular place? Wouldn't His home be *everywhere?*

Our limited understanding concerning this issue is based on what Scripture reveals about the Trinity—one God working through three distinct persons: Father, Son, and the Holy Spirit. Whatever the ultimate answer is, one thing is certain: God the Father, God the Son, and God the Holy Spirit will come and live forever on the new earth, in New Jerusalem.

And I heard a great voice out of heaven saying, Behold, the tabernacle of God is with men, and he will dwell

New Jerusalem

with them, and they shall be his people, and God himself shall be with them, and be their God. (Revelation 21:3)

This truth is an excellent one to use when witnessing to Mormons. The Mormon's polytheistic, three-kingdom view of eternity is refuted in Revelation 21–22. The cult of Mormonism teaches that eternity consists of three kingdoms of God: The celestial, terrestrial, and telestial kingdoms.

The lowest Mormon kingdom is the *telestial,* which happens to be a term the Latter-day Saints have created. But (as Mormon theology teaches), even these lowly telestialmites can advance "by works," through the terrestrial and celestial kingdoms, eventually joining the thousands of other faithful Mormons who have been elevated to godhood. As gods, these Latter-day Saints have copious amounts of celestial sex so they can populate their own planet—a planet they rule over, just as God rules over the earth.

This warped view of eternity does not line up with Scripture. The last two chapters of Revelation specifically teach on eternity, and oddly enough, there is no mention of three kingdoms of God—not one word about a celestial, terrestrial, or telestial kingdom. Scripture is also devoid of references to other planets ruled by Mormon gods and goddesses, neither is there any teaching about man's ability to earn godhood.

What these precious chapters do reveal is that eternity will consist of one eternal kingdom—the new heaven, new earth, and New Jerusalem. God Himself, the only God of the universe, will come and live forever with all His people, "There is no God else beside me; a just God and a Saviour; there is none beside me" (Isaiah 45:21); "I am the first, and I am the last; and beside me there is no God" (Isaiah 44:6).

Angels Will Be There Too!

One heavenly group often overlooked when discussing eternity are God's holy angels. In addition to the Godhead and all the saints, the new earth and New Jerusalem will be inhabited by the vast number of heavenly angels with their different varieties. Living with these faithful, ministering spirits will be a unique experience. The thought of having a chitchat with Michael, Gabriel, or one of the cherubim is most intriguing.

> But ye are come unto mount Sion, and unto the city of the living God, the heavenly Jerusalem, and to an innumerable company of angels. (Hebrews 12:22)

New Jerusalem

Unlike the great cities of history that were built by the ingenuity of man, New Jerusalem is a heavenly city constructed completely by God Himself, "whose builder and maker is God" (Hebrews 11:10). The beauty and majesty of Babylon, Rome, or the huge cities of today pale in comparison to the eternal splendor—the sheer enormity—of what God has created for His people, His angels, and Himself.

> But now they desire a better country, that is, an heavenly: wherefore God is not ashamed to be called their God: for he hath prepared for them a city. (Hebrews 11:16)

Jesus Christ promised that within the walls of New Jerusalem God has built beautiful homes for all of His children. In heaven there will be no marriage, so it is difficult to predict

New Jerusalem

whether or not our present families will live together. There are no Scriptures validating such an idea. If not, I'm sure many of us will request that our loved ones be at least in the same neighborhood.

> In my Father's house are many mansions: if it were not so, I would have told you. I go to prepare a place for you. And if I go and prepare a place for you, I will come again, and receive you unto myself; that where I am, there ye may be also. (John 14:2–3)

Measuring the City

In Revelation 21, an angel carried John to "a great and high mountain" so that he could see the outside of New Jerusalem in greater detail. This angel had "a golden reed to measure the city, and the gates thereof, and the wall thereof" (Revelation 21:15).

A reed was a type of measuring implement used in both Old and New Testament days. It was made from a plant called "calamus," also referred to as "sweet cane." The reed was cut to measure exactly ten and one-half feet. However, the measuring device this angel had was not of plant variety, but mineral. The reed that measured the golden city, "New Jerusalem," was made of gold itself. This proves one thing: Angels are strong—very strong! A solid gold bar ten and one-half feet in length would be mighty heavy. And toting this thing around a city the size of New Jerusalem would take superhuman strength. A word of wisdom to all you arm wrestlers: When in heaven, don't challenge angels!

If you have never heard of the size or read the description of New Jerusalem, then hold on! It's awesome! The city is built "foursquare" (Revelation 21:16), meaning all four sides are equal in length. Each side is 12,000 furlongs. A furlong is 600 Greek feet or 660 English feet. There is a difference of opinion as to how many miles these 12,000 furlongs translate into. I've heard everything from 1,364 miles to 1,500 miles. One thing agreed on is that 12,000 furlongs is a great distance.

What is absolutely uncanny is the fact that the height of New Jerusalem is equal to its sides, "The length and the breadth and the height of it are equal" (Revelation 21:16). This truth may come as a surprise to those who think the new earth is our present earth restored. If this were true, one would need a space suit to explore the eternal city!

Based on 1,500-mile dimensions, the area inside New Jerusalem is 3.3 billion square miles (3,375,000,000). It is difficult to comprehend how tremendously huge this is. Consider this: The mainland area of the United States is approximately 3.5 million square miles. Nine hundred and sixty-four countries the size of the United States could fit inside New Jerusalem, with an extra million square miles left over for good measure. Maybe this is one reason God gives the believer eternal life; it will take us that long just to see the sights of this amazing city!

Revelation 21:17 says the wall of the city is one hundred and forty-four cubits. A cubit is eighteen inches which was established upon the average length of a man's forearm from elbow to fingertip. One hundred and forty-four cubits equals 216 feet. Although Scripture doesn't say whether this measurement represents the height or thickness of the wall, we can logically assume it refers to the thickness.

Revelation 21:12 states that the wall is, "great and high." If you and I were standing at the base of a wall 216 feet high, it would indeed seem great and high. However, in relation to a city that is 7,920,000 feet high, 216 feet would be microscopic. With this book in hand, stand up for a moment. Are you

New Jerusalem

standing? Now, let's say you were going to build a wall around yourself. Would you build the wall in relation to "your height," or to the height of a small flea? John, after seeing a city almost eight million feet high, would not then look at a wall 216 feet high and call it "great and high." Obviously, the wall surrounding New Jerusalem is as high as the city itself. The measurement of 216 feet has to represent its thickness.

The Gates of the City

New Jerusalem will have twelve entrance gates—three on each of its four sides, "On the east three gates; on the north three gates; on the south three gates; and on the west three gates" (Revelation 21:13). If equally dispersed, there would be 500 miles between each gate.

In heaven there must be gigantic oyster beds, producing the largest and finest mother-of-pearl, for each gate is made entirely of one pearl, "And the twelve gates were twelve pearls; every several gate was of one pearl" (Revelation 21:21).

Inscribed on each of these twelve *pearly gates* will be the name of one of the twelve tribes of Israel. If God used His wilderness tabernacle as the blueprint for these gates, the names will appear as follows:

East side
First gate: Judah
Second gate: Issachar
Third gate: Zebulun

South side
Fourth gate: Reuben
Fifth gate: Simeon
Sixth gate: Gad

West side
Seventh gate: Ephraim
Eighth gate: Manasseh
Ninth gate: Benjamin

North side
Tenth gate: Dan
Eleventh gate: Asher
Twelfth gate: Naphtali

The Levites are not numbered with the twelve tribes of Israel because they were priests who constantly moved from camp to camp performing their priestly duties. The twelve gates with the names of the tribes of Israel will be an eternal reminder to Gentile believers that it was through the twelve tribes—and finally through Jesus, "the Lion of the tribe of Judah"—that we entered faith.

The twelve *pearly gates* of New Jerusalem will have angelic receptionists greeting folks as they travel in and out of the holy city.

> And [New Jerusalem] had a wall great and high, and had twelve gates, *and at the gates twelve angels*, and names written thereon, which are the names of the twelve tribes of the children of Israel. (Revelation 21:12)

Twelve Foundation Theory

> And the wall of the city had twelve foundations, and in them the names of the twelve apostles of the Lamb. (Revelation 21:14)

The great wall surrounding New Jerusalem has twelve foundations. These foundations could form the base of the 500 miles of wall between each gate. This is a logical conclusion, but I'd like to stir the gray matter a bit and propose another possibility.

When walking into certain buildings such as cathedrals, one cannot help but notice the headroom. I mean, fifteen NBA centers stacked upon one another would not reach the ceiling in some of these structures. While appreciating the architectural beauty, I've often thought, *What a waste of room!*

New Jerusalem

My theory concerning the foundations of New Jerusalem is based upon the premise that God would not build a one-floor city with over a thousand miles of empty overhead. Theoretically, New Jerusalem could have twelve levels. If these levels were equally separated, each would be 125 miles high and 1,500 miles long and wide. Each of these levels would be named after one of the twelve apostles.

At first, this theory may sound a little strange, but then there has never been a city like New Jerusalem. When we think of a skyscraper, the image that comes to mind is a tall building with one foundation and many ascending floors. However, the concept of floors in tall buildings cannot be compared to the unique design of a city built by God; a city where each of the twelve levels would be 1,500 miles long, 1,500 miles wide, and 125 miles high. It would take a support system unknown to man, but these twelve support systems could appropriately be called *foundations*.

Whether the twelve foundations are intervals between the gates, or twelve levels equally divided in the 1,500 mile height of the city, God bestows great honor on the twelve apostles by printing their names upon these foundations, "and in them the names of the twelve apostles of the Lamb" (Revelation 21:14).

The Foundations of Faith

In Ephesians 2, we learn that Gentiles were once foreigners to the promises of God. But Jesus Christ, through His atonement, broke the partition—the supernatural barrier that separated the Jew from the Gentile. This means everyone can become members of the household of God—a household that is "built upon the foundation of the apostles and prophets, Jesus Christ himself being the chief corner stone" (Ephesians 2:20).

The twelve apostles, through Jesus Christ, are the foundations of New Testament faith. These anointed men boldly went out into a hostile world and established Christianity as the only door into the eternal kingdom of God. Because of their faithfulness and willingness to even die for the cause of *truth*, their names will forever be indelibly written upon New Jerusalem.

The twelve foundations of New Testament faith will eternally be the banner upon the twelve foundations of New Jerusalem!

The Twelve Foundations

Having been personally involved with lapidary work, I find the material God used for the foundations of New Jerusalem quite fascinating. Our homes are generally built upon cement, but the wall of God's eternal city is based upon precious and semiprecious stones. The following is a list of the twelve foundations, the material they are made of, and the name of an apostle. There is no way of knowing the order in which the apostles will appear; so I will list them according to Acts 1:

First foundation: The apostle Peter *Jasper*—jasper is a mixture of quartz and iron oxide. The colors of jasper are white, red, yellow, brown and black. These colors are often swirled together forming beautiful pictures.

Second foundation: The apostle James *Sapphire*—the sapphire is a transparent gem. Sapphires are usually blue due to impurities (iron and titanium). However, they can be found in practically any color. The red ones are called rubies.

Third foundation: The apostle John *Chalcedony*—chalcedony is a term used for a variety of agates. The chalcedony used for the third foundation will more than likely be pure chalcedony. The pure variety is a cloudy looking

New Jerusalem

semitransparent white agate. The name comes from a town in Turkey, Chalcedon, where the mineral was first mined.

Fourth foundation: The apostle Andrew *Emerald*—the emerald is a rich green precious gemstone. Emeralds (especially large ones) rival diamonds in value. The finest emeralds in the world come from Colombia.

Fifth foundation: The apostle Philip *Sardonyx*—sardonyx is a combination of sard and onyx. The colors are brown, gold, and bloodred. This stone is at its most beautiful when it is crosscut against its banded fortification.

Sixth foundation: The apostle Thomas *Sardius*—sardius, better known as carnelian, is a beautiful orange-red agate. Besides the usual orange-red color, carnelian can be found in bloodred and brownish red. Some of the highest quality carnelian I've seen is found only fifty miles south of where I live in the state of Washington.

Seventh foundation: The apostle Bartholomew *Chrysolyte*—the mineral chrysolyte, in the form of a gemstone, is called olivine or peridot. This transparent gem is yellowish green in color.

Eighth foundation: The apostle Matthew *Beryl*—beryl crystals range from one-fourth inch to twelve inches in diameter, although rare specimens of up to eighteen feet have been found. Beryl comes in different colors, both opaque and transparent, but the variety most sought after is the rich green gemstone, emerald. Pure beryl, which is colorless, was once used for eyeglasses.

Ninth foundation: The apostle James (son of Alphaeus) *Topaz*—topaz is an extremely hard gemstone. It is ranked eighth on Mohs' scale of hardness and will scratch quartz. The rarest and most highly valued stone is the golden topaz. The most common colors are blue, white, rich yellow, light brown, and pinkish red.

Tenth foundation: The apostle Simon *Chrysoprasus:* chrysoprase is an apple-green gemstone. Today, chrysoprase is found only as a transparent stone. However, it is said in Old Testament times the apple–green color was impregnated with beautiful gold spots. I'm hoping God used the gold spot variety for the tenth foundation.

Eleventh foundation: The apostle Jude (brother of James) *Jacinth*—jacinth, also called hyacinth, is both a gemstone and a flowering plant. Jacinth is a silicate of zirconia (zircon) and is found in either an orange-red or red-brown color.

Twelfth foundation: The apostle Matthias *Amethyst*—amethyst is a gemstone of purple or bluish-violet color. Because of its availability, it is one of the more inexpensive gemstones. The ancient Greeks believed wearing amethyst protected ône from becoming intoxicated.

The wall between each of these foundations is made of jasper. Here on earth all varieties of jasper are opaque, but heavenly jasper, the variety used on New Jerusalem's wall, will probably be translucent, "having the glory of God: and her light was like unto a stone most precious, even like a jasper stone, clear as crystal" (Revelation 21:11).

> And the building of the wall of it was of jasper: and the city was pure gold, like unto clear glass. (Revelation 21:18)

God's Glory Fills the City

New Jerusalem is a heavenly golden city, "the city was pure gold, like unto clear glass...and the street of the city was pure gold, as it were transparent glass" (Revelation 21:18, 21). The streets of New Jerusalem are gold, the buildings are gold, and our heavenly mansions are gold—but not like the kind

New Jerusalem

purchased at the local jeweler. This gold is so pure, it is transparent. But why? Why would God create a translucent city? I believe there can only be one answer: So God's *Shekinah* glory can illuminate every square inch! Moses tasted this Shekinah glory on Mount Sinai when He asked God to show him His glory (Exodus 33:18).

> And it shall come to pass, while my glory passeth by, that I will put thee in a clift of the rock, and will cover thee with my hand while I pass by: And I will take away mine hand, and thou shalt see my back parts: but my face shall not be seen. (Exodus 33:22–23)

When Moses came down from Mount Sinai, the Hebrews were actually afraid to approach him because his face glowed with the Shekinah glory of God.

New Jerusalem will have no electrical power plants, no gas guzzling generators, and no artificial lighting systems. The divine glory of God and Christ will light up the entire city.

> And the city had no need of the sun, neither of the moon, to shine in it: for the glory of God did lighten it, and the Lamb [Jesus Christ] is the light thereof. (Revelation 21:23)

New Jerusalem will not be a city of shadows, for God's light will be everywhere. Mere words cannot express how wonderful it will be living, walking, and fellowshipping in God's glory. Magnificent? Glorious? Breathtaking? Awesome? Much too weak! No man-made superlatives could describe the eternal glory, beauty, and majesty of New Jerusalem.

HAND GUIDE TO THE FUTURE

The River of Life

The last chapter of the last book of the Bible begins with the angel taking John inside New Jerusalem. The first thing he sees is the river of life. This mighty river probably meanders throughout New Jerusalem, which would make it the longest river ever. The possibility exists it may also flow out of New Jerusalem, supplying water to the new earth. This could be accomplished through thousands of tributaries branching out then eventually emptying back into the main flow. If this is true, it brings up two interesting questions:

1. How could one river's source supply enough water to an earth probably a lot larger than our present earth?

No ordinary river could perform such a task, but the headwaters of the river of life come from no ordinary source. The eternal river flows directly from the throne of God and Christ, "And he shewed me a pure river of water of life, clear as crystal, proceeding out of the throne of God and of the Lamb" (Revelation 22:1). Unless I'm missing something, the throne of God and Christ continuously creates water for the everlasting river.

2. The new earth will have no sea (Revelation 21:1), so what will this river empty into?

That is a tough question. Maybe God will pump water from His throne much as our hearts pump blood through our bodies. God's throne could both create and circulate the water.

The believer will be privileged to drink from this river, "Let him that is athirst come. And whosoever will, let him take the water of life freely" (Revelation 22:17). This powerful verse is given to those in New Jerusalem to quench their thirst and to those today who have no hope in finding anything better than what life has dealt them. It is as if our Savior says, "Come and

New Jerusalem

drink of Me, for I am the headwaters of faith. Freely drink of Me, and you will never thirst again. Your parched soul will become irrigated with the promise of eternal life. Your faith will become the fertile soil in which God graciously plants His love, joy, peace, and hope." Folks, this is a "steal of a deal!"

> In the last day, that great day of the feast, Jesus stood and cried, saying, If any man thirst, let him come unto me, and drink. He that believeth on me, as the scripture hath said, out of his belly shall flow rivers of living water. (John 7:37–38)

The Tree of Life

John saw the tree of life on both sides of the river of life, "In the midst of the street of it, and on either side of the river, was there the tree of life." Some believe that New Jerusalem will have only one tree of life since "tree" is singular. But Revelation 22:2 clearly indicates that John saw two trees, one on each side of the river.

It is my opinion that the entire river will be lined with these trees. Why? I'm glad you asked! Revelation 22:2 goes on to say, "the tree of life, which bare twelve manner of fruits, and yielded her fruit every month." The tree of life is in New Jerusalem (probably outside the city limits as well) to serve those who live on the new earth. With millions of people in the city at any given time, one tree just wouldn't do the job. It would give a whole new meaning to the very thing we all hate to do: stand in line!

These fantastic trees will yield twelve varieties of fruit—a different kind each month of the year. If these trees of life are identical to the one in the Garden of Eden, the fruit will contain life-preserving qualities. The parents of mankind, Adam and Eve, needed to eat from this tree in order to sustain eternal life. After the fall, God took away their access to the tree by placing at least two cherubs on guard duty.

> So he drove out the man; and he placed at the east of the garden of Eden Cherubims, and a flaming sword which turned every way, to keep the way of the tree of life. (Genesis 3:24)

Not being able to eat from the tree, Adam and Eve lived long lives, but they eventually died.

Not only will saints enjoy the twelve varieties of fruit, but they will also use the leaves of the trees, "and the leaves of the tree were for the healing of the nations" (Revelation 22:2). The Greek word for "healing" is *therapeia,* which has two diverse meanings: "health" or "household." Our glorified bodies will be in a state of constant health; not susceptible to sickness or disease. This would seem to preclude a "health" interpretation. If this line of reasoning is correct, Revelation 22:2 could accurately be paraphrased, "and the leaves of the tree were for the *households* of the nations." The leaves of the tree would be used in an industrial fashion serving the households of those who live upon the new earth. Possible uses could be clothing, cooking spices, cleaning agents, and things of this sort.

Developing the New Earth

There are no Bible verses that say, "Ye shall go out and develop the new earth," but its development is a logical assumption. Think about it: God will not only create a new universe, He will also create a new earth—a heavenly earth probably many times larger than our present earth. It's inconceivable to think believers will be confined to the eternal city, never venturing out to explore and develop the new earth.

New Jerusalem would not have twelve gates and twelve angelic receptionists if traffic wasn't to be entering and exiting. Also, Revelation 21 tells us the new earth will have nations.

> And the nations of them which are saved shall walk in the light of it: and the kings of the earth do bring their glory and honour into it...And they shall bring the glory and honour of the nations into it. (Revelation 21:24, 26)

Each believer is promised a mansion in New Jerusalem. The Christian will definitely spend a great deal of time in this marvelous city: exploring its vastness, eating from the tree of life, drinking from the river of life, fellowshipping with one another, and worshipping before the throne of God and Christ. At the same time, it will be exciting going out and developing a whole new world—building cities and nations. The new earth will be an equal opportunity employer: plenty of work for everyone!

What will make the development of the new earth an extremely enjoyable task is the fact that God's new creation will not suffer the repercussions of the curse He placed upon this present earth.

No More Curse

When Adam and Eve disobeyed God's direct command not to eat of the Tree of the Knowledge of Good and Evil, two significant events occurred: They lost access to the tree of life; and God smote the earth with a curse, "Cursed is the ground for thy sake; in sorrow shalt thou eat of it all the days of thy life;

thorns also and thistles shall it bring forth to thee" (Genesis 3:17–18). Everything linked to this curse has plagued mankind from the book of Genesis to the last two chapters of the book of Revelation, when God creates a new universe and earth. The heavenly earth will be curse free!

How truly wonderful it will be living in a world that is free of sin, Satan, demons, sickness, and disease; a world where the gardener will not have to contend with weeds, bugs and slugs; where special outings, such as *picnics*, will not be invaded by pesky ants, mosquitos, gnats, flies, or wasps.

The new earth will also be free of the natural disasters that continually smite our present earth. You will never hear an ominous broadcast warning people about a deadly flood, hurricane, tornado, or earthquake. These natural calamities will not occur on the heavenly earth.

We live in a world that demands decay and death; where physical laws enforce such things as *entropy*. Entropy (or the second law of thermodynamics), means that order always deteriorates to disorder. A new home, left to itself, deteriorates over time. You buy a car and immediately it begins to age. But just as a believer's natural body will pass away and be replaced with a spiritual body—this natural earth will pass away and be replaced with a spiritual earth where the natural laws of decay and death will not exist.

The fact that order will not deteriorate to disorder will have wonderful ramifications for those developing the new earth. It means both physical and societal degradation will never occur. When houses, factories, and cities are built, they will forever stay new. Not only that, but the purest moral and ethical standards will always be practiced, resulting in everlasting governmental harmony. Nations shall live in peace, and citizens will continually walk in the power, love, and righteousness of God.

New Jerusalem

We can accurately and enthusiastically sum it up like this: The new universe, the new earth, and New Jerusalem—will indeed be an eternal paradise!

Outside Are Dogs

Revelation 21:24, 27; 22:15—are verses used to establish two erroneous teachings: First, there will be unsaved people on the new earth. Second, the verses pertain to the Millennium. I'll address these false-teachings in order.

> Blessed are they that do his commandments, that they may have right to the tree of life, and may enter in through the gates into the city. *For without are dogs, and sorcerers, and whoremongers, and murderers, and idolaters, and whosoever loveth and maketh a lie.* (Revelation 22:14–15)

There will be unsaved people on the new earth: There cannot possibly be unsaved people on the new earth. Eternity with God and Christ is reserved for Christians. The separation between the righteous and unrighteous takes place at the Great White Throne Judgment, where not just a few, but *all* unbelievers will be sent to eternal hell—not to the eternal earth.

> And whosoever was not found written in the book of life was cast into the lake of fire. (Revelation 20:15)

Do you remember what Isaiah 65:17 said? "For, behold, I create new heavens and a new earth: and the former shall not be remembered, nor come into mind." On the new earth, God will not allow the stains of sin and rebellion from the old earth to corrupt the consciousness of His people. But if sinful, unregenerate man were upon the new earth, sin would be in the minds of His children each and every day. No, eternity with God is a reward only for blood-bought, born-again saints!

The verses pertain to the Millennium: I can accept the idea that during the Millennium glorified saints may have access to New Jerusalem—going into heaven every now and then as a refresher. However, the last two chapters of Revelation deal specifically with the new heaven, new earth, and New Jerusalem. The subject is "eternity," not the thousand-year millennial period.

Notice what Revelation 22:15 says, "For without are dogs, and sorcerers, and whoremongers, and murderers, and idolaters, and whosoever loveth and maketh a lie." This is not a description of the millennial period. The Millennium will be a time when Christ and the saints bring peace, restoration, and righteousness to the earth. The Lord and glorified believers will rule "with a rod of iron" (Revelation 2:27; 19:15). Witchcraft, sorcery, prostitution, murder, and pagan worship (i.e., the sins listed in Revelation 22:15) will not be tolerated. For a very short time at the end of the Millennium, Satan will be loosed to deceive the nations. However, during the Millennium itself, Jesus Christ will have complete control and authority.

The sorcerers, whoremongers, murderers, and idolators of Revelation 22:15 are those *outside* New Jerusalem—outside the new earth and outside eternal life with God. They are *inside* a place called hell.

The choice is ours, man's will is free, heaven or hell—which will it be?

Behold, I Knock at the Door

God has given us just a small taste of what to expect in heaven. But the sad truth is, if you have been riding the sleepy

New Jerusalem

horse of procrastination. If you have not made a sincere decision for Jesus Christ—all these marvelous things concerning eternity do not pertain to you.

Many people seem to have iron bars and padlocks on their hearts. But if you have made it this far in *Hand Guide to the Future*, I believe you are ready to make the wisest decision a person can make. Jesus said in Revelation 3:20, "Behold, I stand at the door, and knock: if any man hear my voice, and open the door, I come in to him, and will sup with him, and he with me." The door at which Jesus stands is the door to your heart. But there is something rather unique about this door. It can only be opened from one side—your side! Jesus will never force you, nor anyone else, to accept His love, guidance, peace, or His eternal inheritance. The Lord is knocking. It is up to you to open the door.

Words don't mean anything unless they are said with sincerity. So don't just read the following words; say them to Jesus and really mean them.

Dear Lord,

The door to my heart is open. Please come in and be my Savior and my best friend. Where there is doubt, give me faith. Where there is fear, give me peace. Where there is pain, give me healing. Forgive me of all my sins, and help me become what You want me to be. Jesus, I don't want cold boring religion, but instead a vibrant love relationship with You, Your people, and Your Word.

I now confess that I am a child of God! I now proclaim that I am born again! Amen.

Welcome to the kingdom of God!

Chapter Eleven

PRETRIBULATION RAPTURE

Critiquing the Rapture Positions

The final chapters of this book will critique the three premillennial rapture positions: pretribulation, midtribulation, and posttribulation. Not all perspectives and concepts will be covered, for the intent is not to be exhaustive, but to demonstrate that worthy arguments can be made for each position.

Rapture positions are often taught from the pulpit with such dogmatism that they tend to inculcate negative feelings in the minds of believers toward the other views. Many Christians

Pretribulation Rapture

give blind allegiance to a particular rapture position without the slightest understanding of what the opposing views are established upon. It's good to take an honest stand on issues: A man who doesn't stand for something, will fall for anything! But an "honest stand" is one based upon fair evaluation of all sides.

One view not included in this critique is the "partial rapture" belief. The author finds this elitist position, which is based on a pretribulation rapture, very weak. Proponents of a partial rapture put some Christians (namely, themselves) into a higher class than other believers. This perfected "higher class" is thought to deserve to be raptured, while the rest of us yo-yos must be purged of our imperfections by being "spanked" by God through the Great Tribulation.

The question the partial rapturist has difficulty answering is, What criteria elevates a Christian into this upper echelon? If it is absolute perfection, then no one will be raptured, for we all sin and fall short of the glory of God. Absolute perfection is an unattainable goal. If it is partial perfection, who sets the standards? How is one to know if he or she has crossed the invisible line of worthiness? The self-righteous egotism on which this belief is founded violates the equality of saints. It also throws the balance between faith, works, and grace out of kilter.

There is nothing wrong with taking a strong stand on a rapture position as long as one is willing to concede the following points:

1. Good arguments can be made for the other positions.
2. This is a nonessential issue.
3. The particular position one holds could possibly be wrong.

Wise Christians put their rapture positions in subjection to a "pan-rapture" perspective—however it "pans out" is fine with them. We should all prepare ourselves to go through the Great Tribulation, but even the diehard posttribulationist will not complain if Jesus raptures His church sooner. Let's plant our lives firmly in faith, commitment, servitude, and God's Word— and keep our eyes looking for that glorious "blessed hope."

Pretribulation Rapture

In today's church, the predominate view of the rapture in relationship to the Great Tribulation is the pretribulation position. Even a cursory look at contemporary books on prophecy indicates the prevalence of this view. Believing that the church will be removed from the earth prior to the cataclysmic judgments of God is by far the most comfortable and easy to accept position. And to the proponents, the most logical. In his book, *Prophecy for Today*, J. Dwight Pentecost made the following comment in support of a pretribulation rapture:

> What is the next event in God's prophetic program? Some are expecting the Tribulation; some are anticipating Armageddon; some are looking for the Beast and the False Prophet. Had that been the anticipation of the apostle Paul, he hardly could have written concerning "the blessed hope and the glorious appearing of the great God and our Savior, Jesus Christ," for it gives one no joy to think of living through the conflagration of Armageddon, nor is it a blessing to anticipate life under the iron fist of the Beast. That event set before the believer, for which we are looking, is the translation or rapture of the Church.[1]

Pretribulation Rapture

Escaping God's Wrath

To the pretribulationist it is inconceivable to rationalize a loving, caring God forcing His beloved children to endure the pain, sorrow, and terror of His wrath for seven years—living under the persecuting murderous reign of the Antichrist, "for God hath not appointed us to wrath, but to obtain salvation by our Lord Jesus Christ" (1 Thessalonians 5:9).

In the following verses the apostle Paul makes a distinction between those who deserve God's wrath, and those who don't.

> But of the times and the seasons, brethren, ye have no need that I write unto you. For yourselves know perfectly that the day of the Lord so cometh as a thief in the night. For when *they* shall say, Peace and safety; then sudden destruction cometh upon *them*, as travail upon a woman with child; and *they* shall not escape. But *ye, brethren*, are not in darkness, that that day should overtake *you* as a thief. (1 Thessalonians 5:1–4)

Notice that the personal pronouns *they* and *them* represent people who are not saved. These are the ones who will be punished throughout the Great Tribulation period: for when *they* shall say Peace and safety; then sudden destruction cometh upon *them*—and *they* shall not escape.

The escapees, the ones who will be raptured, are represented by the personal pronouns *ye—you*, and by the noun *brethren*: "but *ye, brethren*, are not in darkness, that that day should overtake *you* as a thief."

In Luke 21, we see the same truth being expressed. The Great Tribulation is designated for unrepentant sinners, not born-again Christians. In the following verses, Jesus begins with a negative condemning statement directed at a rebellious world, then continues by giving His church a positive redemptive exhortation.

> For as a snare shall it come on all them that dwell on the face of the whole earth. Watch ye therefore, and pray always, that ye may be accounted worthy to escape all these things that shall come to pass, and to stand before the Son of man. (Luke 21:35–36)

Escaping the Trial of Tribulation Saints

Those who subscribe to a pretribulation rapture acknowledge the fact that there will be Christians who will suffer through the Great Tribulation. Therefore a distinction is made between saints who will be translated prior to Daniel's seventieth week and those who are saved after the week has begun (Tribulation saints).

This distinction is used as a rallying initiative for soul-winning. It is applied to inspire Christians to win souls and used as a tool for evangelizing, warning people to refrain from procrastination—to get saved now and avoid becoming a Tribulation saint, which is a born-again believer who is forced to endure God's wrath, Antichrist's persecution, heartache, pain, and even death. Of course, the urgency of faith should be a witnessing issue with all Christians regardless of what they think about the rapture. The Bible says, "Behold, now is the accepted time; behold, now is the day of salvation" (2 Corinthians 6:2). Life can be snatched away from any of us in a split second. And when one is dead, it's too late to keep that faith commitment they were planning on making sometime soon. The road to hell is indeed paved with good intentions.

The twenty-one judgments of God (i.e., the seven seals,

Pretribulation Rapture

seven trumpets, and seven vials) will be His righteous wrath poured out on an ungodly, Christ-rejecting, Antichrist-centered world. The picture of Tribulation saints (people saved during this time) is not a pretty one. Concerning the notorious *mark of the beast*, the Christian will face the old catch-22 syndrome: damned if you do, persecuted and killed if you don't. Taking this infamous mark is tantamount to selling your soul to Satan. It is an unpardonable sin.

> And the third angel followed them, saying with a loud voice, If any man worship the beast and his image, and receive his mark in his forehead, or in his hand, The same shall drink of the wine of the wrath of God, which is poured out without mixture into the cup of his indignation; and he shall be tormented with fire and brimstone in the presence of the holy angels, and in the presence of the Lamb: And the smoke of their torment ascendeth up for ever and ever: and they have no rest day or night, who worship the beast and his image, and whosoever receiveth the mark of his name. (Revelation 14:9–11)

The believer who willfully succumbs to the Antichrist's system by taking the mark of the beast will lose salvation and be eternally condemned to hell. However, for those who refuse the identification mark, life will become hell on earth. Without this mark, a Christian family will not be able to purchase the necessities of life: food, clothing, public utilities, and shelter. Jobs and businesses will be lost and private property confiscated. Eventually, born-again believers will be hunted down and given an ultimatum: Yield to the system and pay homage to the beast (the Antichrist) or die as a martyr.

And he had power to give life unto the image of the

beast, that the image of the beast should both speak, and cause that as many as would not worship the image of the beast should be killed. And he causeth all, both small and great, rich and poor, free and bond, to receive a mark in their right hand, or in their foreheads: And that no man might buy or sell, save he that had the mark, or the name of the beast, or the number of his name. (Revelation 13:15–17)

Pretribers see themselves escaping this oppressive scenario by being raptured before the Great Tribulation begins. Therefore, a distinction is made between *raptured saints* and *Tribulation saints*.

A Two-Stage Second Coming

In his book, *The Beginning of the End*, author Tim LaHaye (a well-known and outspoken proponent of a pretribulation Rapture), teaches that the Second Coming of the Lord is a two-stage event:

The coming of our blessed Lord is to be a two-stage event, and it is separated by a seven-year interval. This seven years is the fulfillment of the "seventieth week" of Daniel, or the time of "Jacob's trouble." This is called the pretribulation view of our Lord's return. [2]

The pretribulation Rapture is actually based on two Second Comings of Jesus Christ: one in the *air*, then seven years later one on *earth*. But since Scripture does not mention two Second Comings, the event is reasoned as two aspects or stages of one Second Coming.

The first stage is a joyous occasion, the blessed hope, when Christ liberates His church from a sinful world that is about to enter the *hour of temptation*, which is the Great Tribulation. This event is called the resurrection and rapture of the church.

Because thou hast kept the word of my patience, I also will keep thee from the hour of temptation, which shall come upon all the world, to try them that dwell upon the earth. (Revelation 3:10)

The second stage of the Second Coming will be both joyous and sad. The church will rejoice in seeing the Antichrist and the False Prophet cast into eternal hell. We will rejoice when Satan is bound in the bottomless pit. We will rejoice seeing Jesus Christ begin His thousand-year reign on earth. But we will also be saddened when we witness the mass extermination of thousands of people who could have traveled God's "narrow road" that leads to heaven, but instead chose the "wide road" that leads to destruction.

Stage one and stage two of the Second Coming are separated by a period of seven years.

Revealing of the Antichrist

Another argument used to support a pretribulation rapture is found in 2 Thessalonians 2, which describes the revealing of the Antichrist. Many believe (myself included) that the revealing of the son of perdition will occur at the beginning of Daniel's seventieth week, when the Antichrist signs a seven-year treaty with the nation of Israel (Daniel 9:27). Pretribulationists believe that the church will be removed from earth before the Antichrist is revealed, thus before the Great Tribulation begins. The text supporting this is 2 Thessalonians 2:3–9.

> Let no man deceive you by any means: for that day shall not come, except there come a falling away first, and that man of sin be revealed, the son of perdition; Who opposeth and exalteth himself above all that is called God, or that is worshipped; so that he as God sitteth in

the temple of God, shewing himself that he is God. Remember ye not, that, when I was yet with you, I told you these things? And now ye know what withholdeth that he might be revealed in his time. For the mystery of iniquity doth already work: only he who now letteth will let, until he be taken out of the way. And then shall that Wicked be revealed, whom the Lord shall consume with the spirit of his mouth, and shall destroy with the brightness of his coming: Even him, whose coming is after the working of Satan with all power and signs and lying wonders. (2 Thessalonians 2:3–9)

Verse 6 reads, "And now ye know what withholdeth that he [the Antichrist] might be revealed in his time." Something is holding back the revealing of the Antichrist, and this something must be removed prior to his revealing. Verses 7 and 8 bear this thought out: "For the mystery of iniquity doth already work: only he who now letteth will let, until he be taken out of the way. And *then* shall that Wicked be revealed."

The words "letteth" and "let" can be substituted with "hinders" and "hinder," or "restrains" and "restrain," so that verse is rendered, "For the mystery of iniquity doth already work: only he who now *restrains* will *restrain*, until he be taken out of the way." The pronoun *he* refers to the one who will be taken out of the way before the Antichrist is revealed.

It is important to note that God did not specify who this "he" is, so the issue is open for debate. Most pretribulationists are certain this "he" is the church. In other words, the church is the force preventing the Antichrist from being revealed. When the church is raptured, the restraining power will be removed, allowing the Antichrist to come forth and radically change the world for the glory of Satan.

Others are equally convinced the "he" in question is the Holy

Spirit who prevents the revealing of the Antichrist. Some pretribulationists counter this argument by saying that the "he" could not possibly be the Holy Spirit because the third person of the Trinity takes an active role in salvation, and many will be saved during the Great Tribulation.

Noah and Lot

In Matthew 24:37 Jesus said, "As it was in the days of Noah, so it will be at the coming of the Son of Man," (NIV). Christ drew a parallel between the antediluvian days of Noah just prior to the great deluge wrath of God and the days preceding His Second Coming. In the days of Noah the human race was in a state of total depravity.

> And God saw that the wickedness of man was great in the earth, and that every imagination of the thoughts of his heart was only evil continually. (Genesis 6:5)

The people of Noah's time were living their lives as though God did not exist. The Creator of all creation, the one to whom they owed everything, didn't occupy a place in their degenerate hearts and minds. Neither did God receive even a resemblant token of appreciation, worship, or praise. They were "eating and drinking, marrying and giving in marriage " (Matthew 24:38); they were sinning, self-centered, thankless, disobedient, and well-deserving of God's terminal judgment. The only God-fearing righteous people on earth were the members of Noah's family. Noah's family can be accurately labeled a *type* of the church.

Just as in the days of Noah, we too live in a godless, selfish, and sinful world. A world that deserves God's wrath. The only righteous ones are those clothed in Christ's righteousness—His church. The pretribulationist questions the mid- and posttribulationists: Are we to believe Noah's family, who are a type of the church, deserved being saved from God's wrath, but the end-time church doesn't?

The same line of reasoning can be used with Lot. Sodom and Gomorrah were two cities steeped in overt malicious sin. Sexual immorality was rampant, and perverted lust was their king. In Sodom large groups of homosexuals roamed the streets, looking for people to molest. Even the two angels that God had sent to Lot were targeted for rape by the men of Sodom.

> Before they had gone to bed, all the men from every part of the city of Sodom—both young and old—surrounded the house. They called to Lot, "Where are the men who came to you tonight? Bring them out to us so that we can have sex with them." (Genesis 19:4–5 NIV)

Lot was the only righteous, God-fearing man in Sodom and Gomorrah, the only one grieved over the moral decadence. So he and his family were granted the opportunity to be saved from God's wrath.

> For if God spared not the angels that sinned, but cast them down to hell, and delivered them into chains of darkness, to be reserved unto judgment; And spared not the old world, but saved Noah the eighth person, a preacher of righteousness, bringing in the flood upon the world of the ungodly; And turning the cities of Sodom and Gomorrah into ashes condemned them with an overthrow, making them an ensample unto those that after should live ungodly; And delivered just Lot, vexed with the filthy conversation of the wicked: (For that righteous man dwelling among them, in

seeing and hearing, vexed his righteous soul from day to day with their unlawful deeds); The Lord knoweth how to deliver the godly out of temptations, and to reserve the unjust unto the day of judgment to be punished. (2 Peter 2:4–9)

God is longsuffering, "not willing that any should perish, but that all should come to repentance" (2 Peter 3:9). But His Spirit will not contend with man forever. Sooner or later the sins must be dealt with and judgment comes. The people in Noah's day had ample time to repent, but they didn't—judgment came! The degenerates in Sodom and Gomorrah had space to repent, but they didn't—judgment came!

God's prophetic Word informs us that this end-time generation will, by and large, refuse to repent and judgment is coming. The Great Tribulation is just beyond the horizon with judgments so fierce that if Jesus didn't intervene, humanity would be annihilated (Matthew 24:22).

The pretribulationist sees a consistent profound truth running through these examples. Noah's family, a type of the church, was saved from the wrath of God. Lot, a type of the church, was saved from the destruction of Sodom and Gomorrah. Likewise, the end-time church will be saved from the Great Tribulation through the rapture.

The Twenty-Four Elders

Just as the New Testament church is commanded to have ruling elders—mature, wise men whose responsibilities are to look after the affairs of the church—heaven will also have a presbyterial order. These heavenly elders are mentioned several times in the book of Revelation (chapters 4, 5, 7, 11, 14, and 19). When the apostle John received Revelation on the island of Patmos, at one point he was literally taken into heaven where he stood before what appeared to be a beautiful, crystalline sea of glass. John saw the magnificent throne of God. He also saw that God's mighty throne was surrounded by twenty-four smaller thrones. These twenty-four thrones are for the twenty-four heavenly elders.

The criteria by which God selects these elders is not known. The overwhelming consensus among Bible scholars is that the twenty-four elders will be comprised of both Old and New Testament figures.

> And round about the throne were four and twenty seats: and upon the seats I saw four and twenty elders sitting, clothed in white raiment; and they had on their heads crowns of gold. (Revelation 4:4)

The pretribulationist would say logic demands that these twenty-four men have been resurrected, raptured, and glorified since they have taken their position as heavenly elders. They are wearing clothes, "clothed in white raiment," and have received their reward, "on their heads crowns of gold." The point is, these heavenly elders are seen in heaven in Revelation 4, before the Great Tribulation begins. They are in heaven before the first seal is opened. If the heavenly presbytery is in heaven before the Great Tribulation, then the church must be there too.

Church Not on Earth during the Great Tribulation

One of the strongest arguments presented for a pretribulation rapture is that the Bible does not depict the church on earth during the Great Tribulation. In Revelation 1:19, Jesus instructs the apostle John to, "write the things which thou hast seen, and the things which are, and the things which shall be hereafter." This is a key verse in putting the book of Revelation in proper context. John is told to write about things *past*, things *present*, and things *future*.

Revelation 1 covers "the things which thou hast seen." Chapters 2 and 3 cover "the things which are." And Revelation 4 through 22 covers "the things which shall be hereafter." Since Revelation is a prophetic book, it stands to reason that the brunt of it (chapters 4 through 22) is prophecy oriented.

The church can be clearly seen in the New Testament, all the way from Matthew through Revelation 3. However, following Revelation 4, the church cannot be seen, it is not mentioned, neither is the word *church* used. The functioning body of Christ (His church) is not on earth during the rise of the Antichrist. It is not on earth during the wrath of God poured out through the seven seals, seven trumpets, and seven vials. The church cannot be seen on earth until Revelation 19, when the saints return with Christ and establish a kingdom of righteousness for a thousand years.

Some pretribulationists believe John being taken into heaven in Revelation 4 represents the rapture of the church. And the twenty-four elders seen by John represent the church in heaven prior to the Great Tribulation.

This ends the pretribulation rapture critique. As you can see, good arguments can be made for this position—however, don't cast your ballot yet! We still have the midtribulation and posttribulation views to examine, and they, too, have worthy arguments.

Chapter Twelve

MIDTRIBULATION RAPTURE

Taking the middle ground on issues is generally considered a coward's paradise—a position of passivity and accommodation, having a nonrocka–boatus mentality. For example, on the issue of the existence of God: the atheist would give a bold No! The Christian would give a resounding Yes! The middle-ground agnostic would give a passive Why, I just don't know.

However, mediocrity is not the premise of midtribulationism. It is an objective, noncompromising position held by many fine Bible scholars. Those who adhere to a midtribulation rapture are people who see difficulties in both pre-and posttribulations positions. In the book, *The Rapture*,

Midtribulation Rapture

Gleason L. Archer had this to say about a midtribulation rapture:

> This mediating approach succeeds in avoiding the difficulties of each of the other two theories and also does justice to the two periods of three and a half years each that are mentioned in Daniel 7:25; 9:27; 12:7, 11; and also in Revelation 11:2. Neither the pretribulationists nor posttribulationists have been able to furnish a convincing explanation for this emphasis on the midpoint of Daniel's seventieth week.[1]

While the midtribulationist sees problems with both pre- and posttribulation positions, oddly enough, the pre- and midtribulationists are theological bedfellows concerning many rapture concepts. Contrary to the perception of many pretribers, midtribers use exactly the same Scripture interpretive reasoning for escaping the wrath of God: 1 Thessalonians 5:1–4; 1 Thessalonians 5:9; Luke 21:36; Revelation 3:10; Titus 2:13; and 2 Peter 2:4–9. And arguments against the posttribulation position are virtually identical.

When Does God's Wrath Begin?

When discussing pre- versus midtribulation rapture perspectives, the issue is not escaping the wrath of God, but when does God's wrath begin? The pretribulationist believes God's wrath will begin when the Antichrist signs a seven-year treaty with the nation of Israel. The midtribulationist who accepts a three and one-half year Great Tribulation and a "pre-wrath rapture" believes God's wrath will commence in the middle of Daniel's seventieth week when the infamous treaty is broken and the Antichrist commits the abomination of desolation.

> And he shall confirm the covenant with many for one week: and in the midst of the week he shall cause the sacrifice and the oblation to cease, and for the overspreading of abominations he shall make it desolate, even until the consummation, and that determined shall be poured upon the desolate. (Daniel 9:27)

> When ye therefore shall see the abomination of desolation, spoken of by Daniel the prophet, stand in the holy place, (whoso readeth, let him understand:) Then let them which be in Judaea flee into the mountains: Let him which is on the housetop not come down to take any thing out of his house: Neither let him which is in the field return back to take his clothes. And woe unto them that are with child, and to them that give suck in those days! But pray ye that your flight be not in the winter, neither on the sabbath day: For then shall be great tribulation, such as was not since the beginning of the world to this time, no, nor ever shall be. (Matthew 24:15–21)

The passage from Daniel 9 states that a seven-year covenant will be made with Israel, and that this treaty will be broken after three and one-half years. Then the passage from Matthew 24 refers to this covenant and proceeds to tell Jewish people to flee out of *Judaea* when they see the abomination of desolation.

Notice that verse 21 states, "For *then* shall be great tribulation." And we ask: when will there be great tribulation? The answer is found in verse 15, "When ye therefore shall see the abomination of desolation, spoken of by Daniel the prophet." The abomination of desolation occurs in the "middle" of Daniel's seventieth week. This is when the Great Tribulation begins. This is when the church will be raptured and be saved from the wrath of God.

You see, the midtribulationist divides Daniel's seven years (seventieth week) into two three and one-half year periods. The first three and one-half years begins with the revealing of the Antichrist and his seven-year treaty with the nation of Israel. The second three and one-half years begins with the abomination of desolation, when "Mr. 666" defiles the temple in Jerusalem—which is the key incident triggering God's wrath, called the Great Tribulation.

> Who opposeth and exalteth himself above all that is called God, or that is worshipped; so that he as God,sitteth in the temple of God, shewing himself that he is God. (2 Thessalonians 2:4)

Three and One-Half Year Great Tribulation

The midtribulationist would ask the pretribulationist to take a close look at Scripture in relationship to the Antichrist, Israel, and the wrath of God. Scripture gravitates to a three and one-half year Great Tribulation—not seven years. Think about it: where does the Bible say the Great Tribulation is seven years? Daniel 9:27 certainly doesn't say this. It speaks of a seven-year *covenant* not *Tribulation.* Nowhere in Scripture will you find the Great Tribulation represented by a period of seven years.

> And from the time that the daily sacrifice shall be taken away, and the abomination that maketh desolate set up, there shall be a thousand two hundred and ninety days. (Daniel 12:11) *Three and one-half years*

> But the court which is without the temple leave out, and measure it not; for it is given unto the Gentiles: and the holy city shall they tread under foot forty and two months. (Revelation 11:2) *Three and one-half years*
>
> And the woman fled into the wilderness, where she hath a place prepared of God, that they should feed her there a thousand two hundred and three score days. (Revelation 12:6) *Approximately three and one-half years*
>
> And there was given unto him [Antichrist] a mouth speaking great things and blasphemies; and power was given unto him to continue forty and two months. (Revelation 13:5) *Three and one-half years*

Opening of the Sixth Seal

We have differentiated between the seven-year pretribulation view of the wrath of God and the three and one-half year midtribulationist view. But where in Scripture does the wrath of man (the Antichrist) end and the wrath of God begin? Is Scripture clear on this issue? The midtribulationist believes it is.

We have already seen that the abomination of desolation occurs in the middle of Daniel's seventieth week. We learned that this event triggers the wrath of God. However, there is another interesting passage of Scripture which proves this point from a different perspective—the opening of the sixth seal.

> And I beheld when he had opened the sixth seal, and, lo, there was a great earthquake; and the sun became black as sackcloth of hair, and the moon became as blood; and the stars of heaven fell unto the earth, even as a fig tree casteth her untimely figs, when she is

Midtribulation Rapture

shaken of a mighty wind. And the heaven departed as a scroll when it is rolled together; and every mountain and island were moved out of their places. And the kings of the earth, and the great men, and the rich men, and the chief captains, and the mighty men, and every bondman, and every free man, hid themselves in the dens and in the rocks of the mountains; and said to the mountains and rocks, Fall on us, and hide us from the face of him that sitteth on the throne, and from the wrath of the Lamb: *For the great day of his wrath is come; and who shall be able to stand?* (Revelation 6:12–17)

The opening of the sixth seal introduces the wrath of God. This event would occur simultaneously with the Antichrist invading the temple and committing the abomination of desolation.

The pretribulationist would say that all seven seals are part of God's Tribulation judgments. The midtribulationist would disagree, and point out that seals one through five are not associated with God's wrath.

The first five seals describe the first three and one-half years of Daniel's seventieth week. During this first three and one-half year period, the four horsemen of the apocalypse will come forward to fulfill their purpose; the Antichrist will be revealed and enter into a seven-year treaty with the nation of Israel; and Christians will be persecuted and many will be killed due to their faith and resistance to the harlot system.

When the fifth seal is opened, the souls of martyred saints will cry out to Jesus, "How long, O Lord, holy and true, dost thou not judge and avenge our blood on them that dwell on the earth?" (Revelation 6:10). These slain brethren wanted to know how long before God would unleash His wrath and avenge their blood. They did not have to wait long, for God's wrath begins with the opening of the sixth seal, "For the great day of his wrath is come; and who shall be able to stand?"

The Great Tribulation judgments begin with the opening of the sixth seal, which means the rapture of the church would take place between the fifth and sixth seals.

Revealing of the Antichrist

If the Rapture occurs between the fifth and sixth seals—three and one-half years after the Antichrist has been revealed—how would the midtribulationist counter the pretribulationist's view of 2 Thessalonians 2:3–9? If you will remember, pretribers use this passage to prove that the church will be raptured before the Antichrist is revealed.

I will first reiterate the pretrib view from the "pretribulation rapture critique." This will be followed by three different interpretations held by midtribulationists.

Pretribulation View Revisited

Second Thessalonians 2:6 reads, "And now ye know what withholdeth that he [the Antichrist] might be revealed in his time." Something is holding back the revealing of the Antichrist, and this something must be removed prior to his revealing. Verses 7 and 8 bear this thought out: "For the mystery of iniquity doth already work: only he who now letteth will let, until he be taken out of the way. And then shall that Wicked be revealed."

The words "letteth" and "let" can be substituted with "hinders" and "hinder," or "restrains" and "restrain," so that verse is rendered, "For the mystery of iniquity doth already work: only he who now *restrains* will *restrain*, until he be taken out of the way." The pronoun *he* refers to the one who will be taken out of the way before the Antichrist is revealed.

It is important to note that God did not specify who this "he" is, so the issue is open for debate. Most pretribulationists are certain that this "he" is the church. In other words, the church is the hindering force preventing the Antichrist from being revealed. When the church is raptured, the restraining power will be removed, allowing the Antichrist to come forth and radically change the world for the glory of Satan.

Others are equally convinced the "he" in question is the Holy Spirit, and that it is the Holy Spirit who prevents the revealing of the Antichrist. Some pretribulationists counter this argument by saying that "he" could not possibly be the Holy Spirit because the third person of the Trinity takes an active role in salvation, and many will be saved during the Great Tribulation.

Three Midtrib Interpretations

Let's now examine the three midtribulationist's interpretations of the "revealing" and "he" verses in 2 Thessalonians 2.

Interpretation one: Although the Bible calls Satan "the god of this world" (2 Corinthians 4:4), the most powerful force operating on the earth is the mighty Holy Spirit. To some midtribers it is complete folly to give credit to mere people (i.e., the church) for holding back the satanic power of the Antichrist.

> Even him, whose coming is after the working of Satan with all power and signs and lying wonders. (2 Thessalonians 2:9)

The power Christians have over the devil and demons is not their own. It is the power of the Holy Ghost working through them. Scripture often refers to the Holy Spirit as "he," and it is "he," not the church, that is holding back the revealing.

To address the pretrib comment about the "he" not being the Holy Spirit on the basis that souls will be saved during the Great Tribulation—the midtribulationist who holds to this interpretation would point out that being *taken out of the way* does not mean the Holy Spirit leaves the earth. It doesn't mean His presence will no longer be felt.

Being *taken out of the way* is a direct reference to the Holy Spirit being removed from hindering the rise and revealing of the Antichrist. Let's say you were trying to enter my home by pushing on the front door. However, I'm keeping you out by pushing from the inside. When I step back and allow you to enter, it doesn't mean I left the house. It just means the "restraining power" had been removed.

Interpretation two: The second view held by some midtribers is that the restraining "he" is comprised of both the Holy Spirit and the church. The force holding back the revealing of the Antichrist is the Holy Spirit working through Christ's church.

Midtribulationists who hold this view would agree with interpretation one, that being *taken out of the way* does not necessitate a rapture interpretation. These midtribers believe that both the Holy Spirit and the church will simply be removed from hindering the revealing of "Mr. 666."

Interpretation three: This third view held by some midtribers is a bit complex in the sense that the idea is foreign to many believers. However, it is one that certainly deserves consideration. If you don't grasp the concept upon one reading, by all means give it another.

Midtribulationists who hold to this interpretation agree with pretribulationists about "he" in 2 Thessalonians 2:7 being

Midtribulation Rapture

the church. They believe that the statement being *taken out of the way* is indeed a reference to the rapture.

How this interpretation supports a midtribulation rapture instead of a pretribulation Rapture is most intriguing. These midtribers see two separate revealings of the Antichrist taught in 2 Thessalonians 2. Pretribulationists constantly quote the "revealing" verses in 2 Thessalonians 2:7–8 to substantiate a pretrib rapture. This is done to the neglect of another "revealing" taught in 2 Thessalonians 2:3.

> Now we beseech you, brethren, by the coming of our Lord Jesus Christ, and by our gathering together unto him, that ye be not soon shaken in mind, or be troubled, neither by spirit, nor by word, nor by letter as from us, as that the day of Christ is at hand. Let no man deceive you by any means: for that day shall not come, except there come a falling away first, and that man of sin be revealed, the son of perdition; Who opposeth and exalteth himself above all that is called God, or that is worshipped; so that he as God sitteth in the temple of God, shewing himself that he is God. (2 Thessalonians 2:1–4)

Paul was writing the church at Thessalonica about the rapture, "Now we beseech you, brethren, by the coming of our Lord Jesus Christ, and by our gathering together unto him." Some of these brethren were being thrown into confusion by falsified reports saying that the rapture and subsequent events had already occurred, "That ye be not soon shaken in mind, or be troubled, neither by spirit, nor by word, nor by letter as from us, as that the day of Christ [already happened]."

Although not many today claim the rapture has already occurred, a significant number preach it could happen at any moment. They teach that nothing stands in the way of Christ gathering His church unto Himself. The apostle Paul repudiates this erroneous perception by stating, "...for that day shall not come, except there come a falling away first, and that man of sin be revealed, the son of perdition." Clearly, two events must occur prior to the Second Coming and rapture of the church.

1. *There must first be a "falling away".* The great Christian apostasy occurs when a significant amount of believers are spiritually seduced away from true faith.

> Now the Spirit speaketh expressly, that in the latter times some shall depart from the faith, giving heed to seducing spirits, and doctrines of devils [demons]. (1 Timothy 4:1)

Sadly, we see this apostasy escalating before our very eyes. The proliferation of heretical doctrine in today's church is absolutely mind-boggling. Also, many individuals, many books, and many religious groups mix new age philosophy with Bible theology which produces apostate doctrine. These teachings will play right into the hands of the one known as the False Prophet. This will cause many who profess to be Christian to apostatize into the coming harlot church.

> But there were false prophets also among the people, even as there shall be false teachers among you, who privily shall bring in damnable heresies, even denying the Lord that bought them, and bring upon themselves swift destruction. And many shall follow their pernicious ways; by reason of whom the way of truth shall be evil spoken of. (2 Peter 2:1–2)

2. *The man of sin will be revealed.* The second event that

Midtribulation Rapture

must precede the rapture is the revealing of the Antichrist. Books have been written and speculations abound as to possible Antichrist candidates. However, his identification will be ratified with the beginning of Daniel's seventieth week, when he signs a seven-year treaty with Israel. This covenant with Israel will introduce the Antichrist's *first revealing*—seen in 2 Thessalonians 2:3. The church will witness this historic event and remain on earth for approximately three and one-half more years. The church will see the fulfillment of the first five seals in Revelation 6.

The Antichrist's *second revealing* will occur in the middle of Daniel's seventieth week—seen in 2 Thessalonians 2:8. He will break the seven-year treaty with Israel, and the holy city Jerusalem will be invaded by Antichrist-led Gentiles, "it is given unto the Gentiles: and the holy city shall they tread under foot forty and two months" (Revelation 11:2). Following this Gentile takeover, the Antichrist will be assassinated. He will receive some sort of death blow to his head.

Satan is a counterfeiter who delights in counterfeiting the things of God. It is not surprising that in his "last hurrah" he counterfeits the greatest event in history: the death and resurrection of Jesus Christ. In verses 3, 12, and 14 of Revelation 13, we discover that the world is going to be absolutely awestruck when they see the resurrection of the Antichrist:

Verse 3, "the fatal wound had been healed. The whole world was astonished and followed the beast" NIV.

Verse 12, "whose fatal wound had been healed" NIV.

Verse 14, "the beast who was wounded by the sword and yet lived" NIV.

Scripture informs us that the world will be deceived by the miracle-working power of the False Prophet, "And deceiveth them that dwell on the earth by means of those miracles" (Revelation 13:14). Couple this with the miraculous death and resurrection of the Antichrist, and most people will be duped into believing the Antichrist is exactly who he claims to be.

> Who opposeth and exalteth himself above all that is called God, or that is worshipped; so that he as God sitteth in the temple of God, shewing himself that he is God. (2 Thessalonians 2:4)

Now let's tie the death and resurrection of the Antichrist to his first and second revealings. We will do this by taking a look at Revelation 17:8, which talks about the beast that *was*, and *is not*, and *yet is*.

> The beast that thou sawest was, and is not; and shall ascend out of the bottomless pit, and go into perdition: and they that dwell on the earth shall wonder, whose names were not written in the book of life from the foundation of the world, when they behold the beast that was, and is not, and yet is. (Revelation 17:8)

The beast *was:* This is the Antichrist's first revealing (2 Thessalonians 2:3). He makes a seven-year covenant with Israel, and through approximately three and one-half years (seals one through five), he rises to head a new world order. "And it was given unto him to make war with the saints, and to overcome them: and power was given him over all kindreds, and tongues, and nations" (Revelation 13:7).

The beast *is not:* In the middle of Daniel's seventieth week the seven-year covenant is broken, and the man of sin is murdered. Revelation 17:8 says the Antichrist will "ascend out of the bottomless pit." In order for him to ascend out of this pit, he must first descend into it. Upon death, the soul of the

Midtribulation Rapture

Antichrist goes into the bottomless pit. According to midtribulationists who accept this interpretation, this is the general time in which the church would be raptured.

The beast *and yet is:* Many Bible scholars believe, and I concur, that the king of the bottomless pit (the destroying angel Abaddon–Apollyon) is none other than the king of all demons—Satan (Revelation 9:11).

Satan is the one who resurrects the Antichrist, and after spending time in the bottomless pit, his second revealing (2 Thessalonians 2:8) will be more powerful than his first revealing. Fortunately, Christians will be raptured before he is revealed the second time.

When the Antichrist is revealed for the second time, he will commit the abomination of desolation and God will respond by opening the sixth seal which begins the time known as the Great Tribulation.

A Satan Incarnate Antichrist?

Will the second revealing manifest a Satan incarnate Antichrist? I know it sounds like an episode of the *Twilight Zone,* but the possibility does exist. It is certainly a theory worth considering. Satan is called, "the prince of the power of the air" (Ephesians 2:2). For thousands of years the devil has had the ability to travel at enormous rates of speed through the sidereal and atmospheric heavens. Since he is not omnipresent, Satan has relied upon demonic spirits and the quickness of movement to deceive the world. This all comes to a screeching halt in Revelation 12—the middle of Daniel's seventieth week.

The archangel Michael along with thousands of other angels under his command square off with Satan's demonic kingdom. With the divine power of God working through

Michael's army, Satan will be stripped of his supersonic mobility. He will be cast to the earth.

> And there was war in heaven: Michael and his angels fought against the dragon; and the dragon fought and his angels, And prevailed not; neither was their place found any more in heaven. And the great dragon was cast out, that old serpent, called the Devil, and Satan, which deceiveth the whole world: he was cast out into the earth, and his angels were cast out with him. (Revelation 12:7–9)

We know the devil loses his mobility in the middle of Daniel's seventieth week because Revelation 12:14 tells us that the Jewish people who are fleeing from his wrath are going to be put under divine protection for "a time, and times, and half a time," which is three and one-half years. This fleeing is identical to the fleeing of the Jews after the abomination of desolation takes place. This proves that we are talking about the final three and one-half years of this present age.

Revelation 12:12 says, "for the devil is come down unto you, having great wrath, because he knoweth that he hath but a short time." Satan is infuriated because he has not only lost his mobility, but also realizes he has only three and one-half years to work with. The best way he can accomplish his demonic end-time agenda is to allow his number one man, the Antichrist, to be assassinated. Once dead, the devil has the opportunity to take human form in the person of the Antichrist, and the counterfeit resurrection takes place.

Through the embodiment of the Antichrist, Satan enters the temple in Jerusalem, proclaims himself to be God, and demands worship. When the world worships the Antichrist, whom are they actually worshipping? "And they worshipped the dragon which gave power unto the beast." Following the War of Armageddon, Satan would then leave the Antichrist and be bound in the bottomless pit, while "Mr. 666" and his cohort, the False Prophet, are cast into eternal hell.

Well, that was certainly an interesting theory! We have now completed the midtribulation rapture critique. As with the pretribulationists, the midtribulationists have some strong arguments to support their position. I purposely left out the "seventh trumpet" argument which is held by some midtribulationists because it is a view that is shared with posttribulationists. The seventh trumpet argument will be presented in the posttribulation rapture critique.

Chapter Thirteen

POSTTRIBULATION RAPTURE

The posttribulation rapture is based on the premise that the church will go through the full seven years of Daniel's seventieth week. This perspective rejects the idea of a two-stage Second Coming of Jesus Christ. The posttribulationist coalesces the Second Coming and the rapture into one event.

One of the arguments used by both pretribulationists and midtribulationists against a posttribulation rapture is: Why would a loving, caring God force His children to suffer His wrath? The posttriber would call this an argument that has not been researched, for they, too, believe Christians will be saved from the wrath of God. In the book, *The Rapture*, Douglas J. Moo had this to say:

Posttribulation Rapture

An important conclusion emerges from this discussion of the nature of the Great Tribulation: there is nothing inherent in it that makes it impossible for the church to be present during it. All agree that no true believer will experience the wrath of God (1 Thess. 5:9), but no description of the Tribulation presents it as a time of wrath upon God's people. All agree that the church experiences tribulation—at times severe tribulation—throughout its existence; but no description of the Tribulation indicates that it will involve greater suffering than many believers have already experienced. [1]

All three premillennial rapture positions teach that the believer will escape the wrath of God. How they escape is the point of confliction. Pre- and midtribulationists believe the body of Christ (His church) will escape through the rapture, whereas the posttribulationist believes Christians will receive a seal of divine protection.

Seal of Divine Protection

Throughout Scripture, God has consistently protected His people from divine wrath designated for infidels. A fine example of this is the confrontation between Moses and the Pharaoh of Egypt. When Moses and Aaron filled Pharoah's ears with those four famous words, "Let my people go!" the Egyptian king was not impressed, nor did he feel any obligation or compulsion to "let God's people go!" And so the wrath of God was kindled against Egypt through ten plagues which were poured out in succession:

1. The plague of blood (Exodus 7:14–25)
2. The plague of frogs (Exodus 8:1–15)

3. The plague of lice (Exodus 8:16–19)
4. The plague of flies (Exodus 8:20–32)
5. The plague of livestock (Exodus 9:1–7)
6. The plague of boils (Exodus 9:8–12)
7. The plague of hail (Exodus 9:13–35)
8. The plague of locusts (Exodus 10:1–20)
9. The plague of darkness (Exodus 10:21–29)
10. The plague of the firstborn (Exodus 11:1–10)

Every man, woman, and child throughout the land of Egypt suffered under these judgments—except the Hebrews! The people Moses was sent to deliver were put under divine protection. We see examples of this in the following passages.

> And I will sever in that day the land of Goshen, in which my people dwell, that no swarms of flies shall be there; to the end thou mayest know that I am the Lord in the midst of the earth. And I will put a division between my people and thy people: to morrow shall this sign be. (Exodus 8:22–23)

> And the Lord shall sever between the cattle of Israel and the cattle of Egypt: and there shall nothing die of all that is the children's of Israel. And Pharaoh sent, and, behold, there was not one of the cattle of the Israelites dead. And the heart of Pharaoh was hardened, and he did not let the people go. (Exodus 9:4, 7)

> And the hail smote throughout all the the land of Egypt all that was in the field, both man and beast; and the hail smote every herb of the field, and brake every tree of the field. Only in the land of Goshen, where the children of Israel were, was there no hail. (Exodus 9:25–26)

Posttribulation Rapture

> And Moses said, Thus saith the Lord, About midnight will I go out into the midst of Egypt: And all the firstborn in the land of Egypt shall die, from the firstborn of Pharaoh that sitteth upon his throne, even unto the firstborn of the maidservant that is behind the mill; and all the firstborn of beasts. And there shall be a great cry throughout all the land of Egypt, such as there was none like it, nor shall be like it any more. But against any of the children of Israel shall not a dog move his tongue, against man or beast: that ye may know how that the Lord doth put a difference between the Egyptians and Israel. (Exodus 11:4–7)

Notice that God did not rapture the Hebrew people. They remained in Egypt but were protected from the judgments that afflicted the Egyptians. Likewise, Christians during the Great Tribulation will not be raptured, but instead they will be saved from the wrath of God.

A parallel can be drawn between the blood that God ordered the Hebrews to place on their door frames and the seal of divine protection put on the foreheads of Christians just prior to the Tribulation judgments.

> When the Lord goes through the land to strike down the Egyptians, he will see the blood on the top and sides of the doorframe and will pass over that doorway, and he will not permit the destroyer to enter your houses and strike you down. (Exodus 12:23 NIV)

God made a divine distinction between the Hebrews and the Egyptians. He will also make a distinction between Christians and the rest of humanity during the Great Tribulation. An invisible seal of divine protection placed on the believer's foreheads will distinguish them from everyone else.

The wrath of God is designated for those who do not have this seal. They are the ones who will choose to follow the Antichrist and willfully take his mark and worship his image.

> And the first went, and poured out his vial upon the earth; and there fell a noisome and grievous sore upon the men which had the mark of the beast, and upon them which worshipped his image. (Revelation 16:2)

In Revelation 9:4, we learn that the demonic locusts released under the fifth trumpet are commanded to harm only those who do not have the protective seal of God.

> And it was commanded them that they should not hurt the grass of the earth, neither any green thing, neither any tree; but only those men which have not the seal of God in their foreheads. (Revelation 9:4)

During the time of the Antichrist's new world order Christians will suffer persecution and some will be martyred. However, nowhere does Scripture depict saints being punished by divine cataclysmic judgments. The invisible seal placed on the forehead of the hundred and forty-four thousand Christian Jews (Revelation 7:2–8) and on the forehead of all believers will protect them from God's wrath.

> Come, my people, enter thou into thy chambers, and shut thy doors about thee: hide thyself as it were for a little moment, until the indignation be overpast. For, behold, the Lord cometh out of his place to punish the inhabitants of the earth for their iniquity: the earth also shall disclose her blood, and shall no more cover her slain. (Isaiah 26:20–21)

Posttribulation Rapture

Church on Earth during the Great Tribulation

The pretribulationists believe that the church is not on earth following Revelation 4 and that the church will not physically return to earth until Revelation 19. To substantiate a pretribulation rapture they also point to the fact that the word *church* cannot be found in the book of Revelation past the third chapter—thus proving the church is not on earth during the Great Tribulation.

The posttribulationist takes strong issue with this line of reasoning. The posttribulationist agrees that the word *church* isn't used following Revelation 3. However, the absence of the word *church* doesn't prove a pretrib rapture, and it certainly doesn't prove that the church isn't on earth during the Great Tribulation—neither does it preclude a posttribulation rapture. The word *church* cannot be found in *any* of the rapture verses; yet the pretribulationist has no difficulty identifying the church in these Scriptures.

Let's bring a little common sense to this issue. The word *church* can represent a building, a specific church, or it can refer to the universal body of Christ (i.e., all churches). When Scripture uses terms: saints, believers, brethren, we, and My people—it represents the church regardless if the word *church* is used. To say the *church* cannot be seen during the Great Tribulation is tantamount to saying *saints* cannot be seen—for after all, saints are Christ's church! The posttribulationist uses Scripture to prove that saints (the church) will be on earth during the Great Tribulation. The posttriber not only teaches that saints will be on earth, but that they will be persecuted by the Antichrist and that many will be killed for their faith in Jesus Christ. The following passages of Scripture prove that the church is indeed on earth during the Great Tribulation.

And when he had opened the fifth seal, I saw under the altar the souls of them that were slain for the word of God, and for the testimony which they held: And they cried with a loud voice, saying, How long, O Lord, holy and true, dost thou not judge and avenge our blood on them that dwell on the earth? And white robes were given unto every one of them; and it was said unto them, that they should rest yet for a little season, until their fellowservants also and their brethren, that should be killed as they were, should be fulfilled. (Revelation 6:9–11)

And it was given unto him to make war with the *saints*, and to overcome them: and power was given him over all kindreds, and tongues, and nations. (Revelation 13:7)

I beheld, and the same horn made war with the *saints*, and prevailed against them. (Daniel 7:21)

And he shall speak great words against the most High, and shall wear out the *saints* of the most High, and think to change times and laws: and they shall be given into his hand until a time and times and the dividing of time. (Daniel 7:25)

For your own reference, here are several more verses that prove the church will be on earth during the Tribulation: Revelation 14:12–13; 16:6; 17:6; 18:4; 18:24.

No Distinction between Saints

It was stated in the pretribulation rapture critique, that

Posttribulation Rapture

regarding the Great Tribulation, pretribers put believers into two categories: the raptured saints and the Tribulation saints. In other words, they make a distinction between Christians raptured before the Great Tribulation and Christians who get saved after this grievous time has begun.

A question the posttriber would ask the pretriber is: does Scripture make this distinction between saints? Think about it for a moment. No one knows when the rapture will occur.

> But of that day and that hour knoweth no man, no, not the angels which are in heaven, neither the Son, but the Father. (Mark 13:32)

"God is no respecter of persons" (Acts 10:34), meaning He does not show favoritism toward certain individuals or groups. His children are all treated equally and fairly. Would it be within the parameters of God's fairness if He were secretly to establish a salvation deadline (a day and hour no one knows), then proclaim that people saved prior to this *mystery time* joyfully go to heaven, while the poor Joe who gets saved one second following the *mystery time* is forced to face hell on earth? The posttributionist considers this a man-made concept that violates the clear context of Scripture and militates against the fairness of God.

If there were a distinction between two classes of end-time Christians (the raptured class and the Tribulation class), it stands to reason that this extremely important New Testament truth would appear many times in Scripture. We would expect to find passages demonstrating this distinction. And we would certainly expect to see verses warning people to get saved before a specific deadline to avoid the consequences of being a "Tribulation saint." However, no such verses exist in the Bible.

This can lead us to only one conclusion. There is no

distinction between believers, and there is no pretribulation rapture. Christians living during the Great Tribulation consist of those saved prior to Daniel's seventieth week and those saved after the week has begun.

Distinction between Believers and Nonbelievers

Pertaining to the rapture of the church, Scripture does not differentiate between two groups of saints. Oh, it does talk about the hundred and forty-four thousand Christian Jews and the two witnesses. But speaking of the church in general, saints are not divided into two camps: Camp Rapture and Camp Tribulation.

Christians are Christians, they represent the church, and the church is seen on earth during the Tribulation. The distinction end-time prophecy makes concerning the wrath of God is not between saints, it is between believers and nonbelievers.

The following passage is one we looked at in the pretribulation rapture critique. Pretribulationists use this passage to support a pretrib rapture. Posttribulationists use it to prove that God makes a distinction between believers and nonbelievers, not saints.

> But of the times and the seasons, brethren, ye have no need that I write unto you. For yourselves know perfectly that the day of the Lord so cometh as a thief in the night. For when they shall say, Peace and safety; then sudden destruction cometh upon them, as travail upon a woman with child; and they shall not escape. But ye, brethren, are not in darkness, that that day should overtake you as a thief. Ye are all the children of light, and the children of the day: we are not of the night, nor of darkness. (1 Thessalonians 5:1–4)

Posttribulation Rapture

The wrath of God poured out through the seals, trumpets, and vials will come upon a sinful world "as a thief in the night." Spiritual darkness permeates the hearts and minds of those who have rejected the glorious gospel of Christ. The god of this world, Satan, has effectively blinded the minds of nonbelievers through belief systems, religions, and philosophies that are antithetical to God's will and Word.

> But if our gospel be hid, it is hid to them that are lost: In whom the god of this world hath blinded the minds of them which believe not, lest the light of the glorious gospel of Christ, who is the image of God, should shine unto them. (2 Corinthians 4:3–4)

Just as a thief who robs a home while the family is sleeping, the wrath of God will descend upon an unsuspecting *sleepy* world—a world in which the minds of people have been sedated with lies, a people whose eyes have been closed to the truth.

Those who willfully reject the "helmet of salvation" and the "garments of praise" are the ones in *darkness*. When the Great Tribulation begins, they will not escape the wrath of God. But the *church* is not in *darkness*, and they will escape, "But ye, brethren, are not in darkness, that that day should overtake you as thief." God has graciously forewarned the church about His coming judgments. Christians are not in the dark concerning what will transpire on the earth during the Great Tribulation.

The Lord also explicitly states that His wrath (be it temporal or eternal) is not designated for the believer.

> For God hath not appointed us to wrath, but to obtain salvation by our Lord Jesus Christ. (1 Thessalonians 5:9)

Another passage of Scripture that demonstrates the end-time

distinction between the believer and nonbeliever is found in Luke.

> For as a snare shall it come on all them that dwell on the face of the whole earth. Watch ye therefore, and pray always, that ye may be accounted worthy to escape all these things that shall come to pass, and to stand before the Son of man. (Luke 21:35–36)

Let's sum this section up by saying that prophetic Scripture makes a distinction between believers and nonbelievers. The Bible says nothing about lucky and unlucky saints. Nowhere in Scripture will you find a distinction made between raptured saints and Tribulation saints.

The posttribulationist believes that correlating the verses we read (1 Thessalonians 5:1–4, 9; and Luke 21:35–36) to the rapture, is simply reading into them something that isn't there. The word *escape* should never be construed as another term for "rapture." During the Great Tribulation the church will indeed escape God's wrath by receiving a seal of divine protection. God's Tribulation judgments will pass over the believer like the plagues of Egypt passed over the Hebrews.

A Great Multitude Which No Man Could Number

In Revelation 7, we see a huge number of Christians standing before the throne of God. These are believers who came out of the Great Tribulation.

> After this I beheld, and, lo, a great multitude, which no man could number, of all nations, and kindreds, and people, and tongues, stood before the throne, and before the Lamb, clothed with white robes, and palms in their hands...And one of the elders answered, saying unto me, What are these which are arrayed in white

Posttribulation Rapture

robes? and whence came they? And I said unto him, Sir, thou knowest. And he said to me, These are they which came out of great tribulation, and have washed their robes, and made them white in the blood of the Lamb. (Revelation 7:9, 13–14)

Pretribulationists and some midtribulationists claim this great multitude which no man could number represents those who will be saved during the Great Tribulation. Posttribulationists would counter this interpretation by pointing out that it cannot be reconciled with what Scripture reveals about the heart and attitude of unsaved people during the Great Tribulation.

During the time of God's wrath, the mind of unregenerate man will be in a perpetual state of rebellion against God. People will have been deceived by the miracle-working False Prophet, "And deceiveth them that dwell on the earth by the means of those miracles" (Revelation 13:14). And they will also admire and follow the Antichrist, "The whole world was astonished and followed the beast" (Revelation 13:3 NIV).

Most people living during the Great Tribulation will accept the Antichrist's new socioeconomic system by taking the "mark of the beast." Without this mark it will be extremely difficult for a family to survive. They will not be able to purchase the necessities of life.

And he causeth all, both small and great, rich and poor, free and bond, to receive a mark in their right hand, or in their foreheads: And that no man might buy or sell, save he that had the mark, or the name of the beast, or the number of his name. (Revelation 13:16–17)

Revelation 14:9–11 tells us that taking the mark of the beast is an unpardonable sin. It is a one-way nontransferable ticket to hell. This will definitely limit the number of people saved during the Great Tribulation.

More proof that the number of people saved during the Tribulation will be minimal (comparatively speaking) is found in Revelation 9 and 16. In these passages we learn that although the unsaved comprehend that their sufferings are directly attributed to God's wrath, they still *refuse to repent* and blaspheme His holy name.

> And the rest of the men which were not killed by these plagues yet *repented not* of the works of their hands, that they should not worship devils, and idols of gold, and silver, and brass, and stone, and of wood: which neither can see, nor hear, nor walk: Neither repented they of their murders, nor of their sorceries, nor of their fornication, nor of their thefts. (Revelation 9:20–21)

> And men were scorched with great heat, and blasphemed the name of God, which hath power over these plagues: and they *repented not* to give him glory. And the fifth angel poured out his vial upon the seat of the beast; and his kingdom was full of darkness; and they gnawed their tongues for pain, and blasphemed the God of heaven because of their pains and their sores, and *repented not* of their deeds. (Revelation 16:9–11)

There is no doubt that people will be saved during the Tribulation. We should all thank the Lord for that! However, the innumerable quantity described in Revelation 7:9, "a great multitude, which no man could number," just doesn't support a pretribulation rapture interpretation. There are significantly more Christians standing before God's throne than those saved

Posttribulation Rapture

during the Great Tribulation.

Since posttribulationists reject a pretrib rapture, they see this immense group comprised of a combination of those saved prior to the Tribulation, those saved during the Tribulation, and those who will be martyred. This would truly be "a great multitude, which no man could number."

The Seventh Trumpet

The seventh trumpet argument is a strong agrument used by posttribulationists as well as some midtribulationists. So, except for the conclusion, the rationale is practically identical.

In 1 Corinthians 15:51–52 and Revelation 10:7 two mysteries and two trumpets are mentioned. Posttribulationists believe that there is a direct correlation between these mysteries and trumpets.

> Behold, I shew you a mystery; We shall not all sleep [die], but we shall all be changed in a moment, in the twinkling of an eye, at the *last trump:* for the trumpet shall sound, and the dead shall be raised incorruptible, and we shall be changed. (1 Corinthians 15:51–52)

Paul refers to the resurrection, rapture, and glorification as a "mystery," and this particular mystery of God will occur at the "last trumpet." This end-time generation of ours will experience seven, and only seven, trumpet blasts. Six of these trumpets will bring forth the wrath of God. However, the seventh trumpet, the "last trumpet," accomplishes God's mystery, which is identical to the one the apostle Paul wrote about: the resurrection, rapture, and glorification of the church.

> But in the days when the seventh angel is about to sound his trumpet, the mystery of God will be

accomplished, just as he announced to his servants the prophets. (Revelation 10:7 NIV)

In Revelation 11:15–18, we learn that when the seventh trumpet is sounded, Christ will begin His millennial reign. And we ask, When will Jesus begin His thousand-year reign? At the end of the Great Tribulation! And when does the rapture of the church occur? When the seventh trumpet is sounded at the end of the Great Tribulation!

> The seventh angel sounded his trumpet, and there were loud voices in heaven, which said: "The kingdom of the world has become the kingdom of our Lord and of his Christ, and he will reign for ever and ever." (Revelation 11:15 NIV)

This concludes the posttribulation rapture critique. As with their counterparts, the posttribulationists offer some great arguments to support their position.

The reason for writing this critique of the three premillennial rapture positions has been to demonstrate that good solid arguments can be made for each position. It is my way of countering all the myriads of books, articles, tapes, and sermons whose sole purpose is to prove the superiority of one particular position.

What does the author believe? I believe that a "wise Christian" admits that good arguments can be made for each rapture position. I believe a "wise Christian" understands that this is a nonessential issue and that there is plenty of room for differing opinions. Finally, I believe a "wise Christian" prepares to go through the Great Tribulation, but prays that it happens sooner, because we all want to see our precious Savior—Jesus Christ.

Posttribulation Rapture

In Closing

Thank you for joining me in an exploration of prophetic events God has graciously revealed in Scripture. I strongly recommend that you share *Hand Guide to the Future* with your friends and relatives who have not yet made a decision for Christ. No, they won't be able to identify with everything presented in this book, but Romans 10:17 tells us that "faith cometh by hearing, and hearing by the word of God." Prophetic Scripture is a powerful witnessing tool.

Heavenly Mindedness

Have you ever heard the expression "Some Christians are so heavenly minded, they are of little earthly good"? The individual who coined that phrase must be one of those in the church who are so *earthly minded,* they are of little *heavenly good!*

Biblically speaking, there is no such thing as being too heavenly minded. You see, heavenly mindedness should not be confused with pious religiosity based on asceticism or pseudospiritual snobbery. We can look at a religious sect that isolates itself from society—one with stringent codes of ethics, morality, dress, and behavior—and label them "so heavenly minded, they are of little earthly good." But that would be an inaccurate deduction because "excessive religious legalism" should never be viewed as "heavenly mindedness."

Several years ago I had an interesting conversation with a local store owner. He shared that his neighbor had become too religious, that he had acquired too much "godliness," and this high-octane godliness drove the poor fellow to suicide. Do you see the gross error in phrases like "too much godliness" or "too much heavenly mindedness"? Phrases like these blame God for the irrational behavior of people. I don't think the store owner realized it, but he was actually attacking true Christian commitment by giving the impression that if you serve the Lord with all your heart, He might just respond by giving you "too much of Himself"—which is totally absurd.

God isn't like a bottle of whiskey, with which moderation (as opposed to overindulgence) is the key. The Lord is omniscient and sovereign. He always gives His children what they need: never too much and never too little.

No, a problem in the Christian church isn't too much heavenly mindedness, it's too much earthly mindedness; too much devotion to the world and its glory rather than to God and His. What we are talking about is a serious heart problem, a spiritual degenerative condition of the cardiodevotional tract! In our society, where Satan's snares are lurking behind every bush, it's not difficult for believers to lose sight of their spiritual values—to have their priorities mixed around in a worldly caldron of compromise.

Heavenly mindedness should not be perceived as an aspect or attribute of the Christian, but instead as a complete way of life. Everything we do should be an extension of our relationship with God. The key is to view this life, and this world, with the kind of heavenly mind-set that Jesus and the apostles had.

In John 18:36, Jesus said "My kingdom is not of this world." And in John 15:19, speaking of His church, the Lord said "ye are not of the world." The believer's kingdom is not of this world: the Christian is *in* the world, but not *of* the world. What does this mean? It means that although we reside on the earth, our citizenship is in heaven.

> But our citizenship is in heaven. And we eagerly await a Savior from there, the Lord Jesus Christ. (Philippians 3:20 NIV)

Posttribulation Rapture

This heavenly mind-set is one that leads to spiritual victory! If we live our Christian lives on the premise that we are foreign diplomats representing a heavenly kingdom and our King just happens to be the Creator of the entire universe—we will truly begin to understand what Scripture means when it refers to us as *pilgrims, strangers,* and *aliens* (Hebrews 11:13; 1 Peter 2:11).

Ah, what a beautiful truth this is. As believers accept who they are and why they're here—they no longer are conformed to this world, but are spiritually transformed by the renewing of their minds to God's Word and will (Romans 12:2). As this transformation takes place, the fruits of the Spirit begin to manifest. Christians become a benefit and blessing to both heaven and earth because they have accepted their roles as ambassadors of a wonderful Creator who loves and cares for His creation.

The Savior washed Peter's feet to signify the kind of heart He desires to see in His people—a heart of a servant. Because of godly submission and obedience, a heavenly minded believer has a Holy Spirit-softened heart that prefers others over themselves (Philippians 2:3–4). What we're talking about is the kind of Christian heart that looks for needs in people's lives and, according to ability and wherewithal, endeavors to meet those needs.

Above all, a heavenly minded believer is one who has a burden for souls, because souls are precious—they are eternal. And you know, the perception isn't that witnessing Christ and sharing the good news of the gospel is a duty, but rather a privilege. It is the glorious fire of the Holy Spirit that burns within a Christian's heart, causing him to both will and to do His good pleasure (Philippians 2:13).

Has the world stolen a piece of your heart? Is spiritual apathy robbing you from a complete Christian experience? If so, take this exhortation toward heavenly mindedness to heart. Apply it to your life, and in the span of only a moment, you can begin viewing this life through a brand new pair of "heaven-blessed eyes."

> Since, then, you have been raised with Christ, set your hearts on things above, where Christ is seated at the right hand of God. Set your minds on things above, not on earthly things. For you died, and your life is now hidden with Christ in God. When Christ, who is your life, appears, then you also will appear with him in glory. (Colossians 3:1–4 NIV)

God bless you!

Notes

Chapter One
1. Bill Larson, *Mission America Newsletter* (1990), p. 2.
2. Merrill F. Unger, *Unger's Bible Dictionary* (Moody Press, 1966), p. 396.

Chapter Two
1. Dave Hunt, T.A. McMahon, *The Seduction of Christianity* (Harvest House, 1985), pp. 82–83.

Chapter Three
1. Grant R. Jeffrey, *Armageddon: Appointment with Destiny* (Frontier Research Publications, 1988), pp. 30–31.

Chapter Seven
1. Merrill F. Unger, *Unger's Bible Dictionary* (Moody Press, 1966), p. 245.
2. Henry M. Morris, *The Revelation Record* (Tyndale House, 1983), pp. 416–417.
3. F.C. Cook, *Barnes Notes* (Baker Books), Vol. 5, p. 396.

Chapter Eight
1. Robert W. Faid, *A Scientific Approach to Biblical Mysteries* (New Leaf Press, 1993), pp. 179–180.

Chapter Eleven
1. J. Dwight Pentecost, *Prophecy for Today* (Zondervan, 1961), p. 24.
2. Tim LaHaye, *The Beginning of the End* (Tyndale House, 1972), p. 21.

Chapter Twelve
1. Gleason L. Archer, *The Rapture* (Zondervan, 1984), p. 115.

Chapter Thirteen
1. Douglas J. Moo, *The Rapture* (Zondervan, 1984), p. 176.

HAND GUIDE TO THE FUTURE

Would your friends, relatives, Bible study, church library, or people you're witnessing to benefit from *Hand Guide to the Future?*

ORDER FORM

Please send me _____ copy(ies) of *Hand Guide to the Future* at $10 each. I have included $2 per book for postage and handling.

Quantity Discounts	
4-6 copies	$8 each
7 or more	$7 each
Include a $4 shipping fee.	
Book Stores contact C.C.L.	

Ship my order to:

Name: _____

Address: _____

City: _____

State, Zip: _____

Send check or money order to:

C.C.L. (Christ Centered Living)
5114 Pt. Fosdick Dr., N.W., E-128
Gig Harbor, WA 98335
Phone/FAX: (206) 857-7146